THE CORN IS GREEN

A COMEDY IN THREE ACTS

BY EMLYN WILLIAMS

★

DRAMATISTS
PLAY SERVICE
INC.

A Welsh-English Key
for
The Corn is Green
Translation and Pronunciation
by
Ellis and Ellen Roberts

The Little Theatre of Wilkes-Barre gave a most successful production of THE CORN IS GREEN in the spring of 1945. Because the district in which Wilkes-Barre is situated is populated to a considerable extent by Welsh people and the descendants of native-born Welsh, the production was of particular interest to those who knew Welsh, Welsh singing, and the folk ways of the Welsh people. Many of the actors were Welsh and particular care was exercised to reproduce as closely as possible the local color of the countryside in which the play is laid. The Dramatists Play Service asked Mr. Thomas M. Hicks, President of The Little Theatre of Wilkes-Barre, to prepare for this edition a few suggestions on the pronunciation of Welsh and the following Key, which includes also a translation of the Welsh expressions used in the play. Mr. Hicks passed this request on to Ellis and Ellen Roberts (Mr. Roberts played the part of Morgan) to do this work, and what follows is the result.

We express our deep appreciation to Mr. Hicks, to Ellis and Ellen Roberts, and to The Little Theatre of Wilkes-Barre for their kindness and courtesy.

A few simple combinations learned will help immeasurably in pronouncing Welsh:

one f—v
two f's ff—f
one l—l
two l's ll—ellh (tongue touches roof of mouth. Exhale suddenly.) It is a sort of lisp.

Meaning and Pronunciation of the Welsh in *The Corn Is Green*:

ACT I—SCENE 1

MR. JONES:
". . . Pechudur wyf, y dua'n fyw—'O Uffern!' yw fy nghri; Gostwng dy glust, a'am llefain clyw . . . So-so-sO-la-sO-so!"

3

(Pronunciation)	". . . Pechadeer oov a deean view 'O Uffern' u va n'gree; Gostoong da gleest am llavan clew . . . So-so-so-la-so-so!"
(Translation)	"I am the blackest sinner alive—'Oh Hell' is my cry; Bend your ear and that thou my hear . . . So-so-sO-la-so-so!"
IDWAL:	Sgwelwchi'n dda, d'wi'di torri'r bloda.
(Pronunciation)	Uss gwelichee 'n tha du widi torry ur bloda.
(Translation)	If you please, I cut the flowers.
IDWAL:	Os gwelwchi'n dda, syr, mae Mistar Tomos wedi 'ngyrru i yma ich gweld chi!
(Pronunciation)	Os gwelicheen tha sur, my mistaar Tomos wedee ungeeree imma eech gweld chee!
(Translation)	If you please, sir, Mister Thomas sent me here to see you!
IDWAL:	Diolch yn'faw, syr . . .
(Pronunciation)	Deeolch un vow sur.
(Translation)	Thank you very much (big) sir.
IDWAL:	Tomos-Aneurin-dyma'r cerbyd—dewch i wel'd-fe ddwe-dai wrth y Scweiar-brysiwch!
(Pronunciation)	Tomos-Ann Newrin-dima ur kerbid—dewch e weld-vu-thwe-die-oorth a Squire—brishuch.
(Translation)	Thomas Aneurin, here's the carriage. Come to see. I will tell the Squire, hurry!

ACT I—SCENE 2

ROBBART:	Be mai'n ddeud?
(Pronunciation)	Be mine theyed?
(Translation)	What did she say?
WILL:	Na-beth of Naw-stee.
(Pronunciation)	Naw beth of Nawstee.
(Translation)	There something nasty.
MORGAN:	Cythral uffarn . . .
(Pronunciation)	Kuthrawl uffarn . . .
(Translation)	Devil from hell!
GLYN:	Be hari hi-hi a'i molchi . . .
(Pronunciation)	Be hari he-he i molchee . . .
(Translation)	What's the matter with her, her and her washing?
JOHN:	Pwy sisho molchi . . .
(Pronunciation)	Puee sisho molchee . . .
(Translation)	Who wants to wash?
WILL:	Welso ti'rioed wraig fel ene-
(Pronunciation)	Welso tee reeoid rig vel een?
(Translation)	Did you ever see a woman like that?

4

MORGAN:	Mae'n lwcus na ddaru mi mo'i thrawo hi lawr a'i lladd hi . . .
(Pronunciation)	Mine lookis na tharoo me moi thrawo he lowr ai llath hi . . .
(Translation)	She is lucky I didn't throw her down and kill her.
ROBBART:	Nawn-i drio molchi-dewch hogia-mae'n well nag eistedd yma-dewch . . .
(Pronunciation)	Nown i drio molchee-dewch hogia mine welch nag eestath eema-dewch.
(Translation)	Let's walk—come boys ——It is better than sitting here—come.
GLYN:	Dynna gusan yti Morgan Bach.
(Pronunciation)	Dinna gissann iti Morgan Back.
(Translation)	There's a kiss for you, little Morgan.
ROBBART:	Cymmer yna y corgu fol.
(Pronunciation)	Kimmer ina u corgee fol.
(Translation)	Take that you foolish Cork.
JOHN:	Dynna ateb-i-ti.
(Pronunciation)	Dinna atteb-i-tee.
(Translation)	There's an answer for you.
WILL:	Jobin da y diawl.
(Pronunciation)	Jobin da u diowl.
(Translation)	A devil of a good job.
MORGAN:	Cai da geg.
(Pronunciation)	Ki da geg.
(Translation)	Shut your mouth.
GLYN THOMAS:	Be'di'r gloch, Merry?
(Pronunciation)	Be deer gloch, Merry?
(Translation)	What time is it, Mary?
1ST GIRL:	Chwarter i bump.
(Pronunciation)	Chwarter ē bimp.
(Translation)	Quarter to five.
A BOY:	W'n i ddim yn wyr-gofyn iddi-
(Pronunciation)	Un e thim un weer govin ithi.
(Translation)	I don't know honestly, ask her.
AN OLD LADY:	Pnawn dydd Iau, te, hanner awr wedi tri-
(Pronunciation)	Pnown dith yi te hanner owr wedi tri.
(Translation)	Thursday afternoon, isn't it, half past three.
IDWAL:	Dyma'r fistress!
(Pronunciation)	Dimar vistress!
(Translation)	Here's the Mistress!
SARAH PUGH:	Mi ddylaswn fod yn pobi heddyw- A dwidi gadal y cig yn y popdy-
(Pronunciation)	Me the lassum vod un pobee hethu- A dwidi gadal u keeg in a pobdee.

5

(Translation)	I should be baking today And I left the meat in the oven.
A MOTHER:	Mi fydd eich cegin chi ar dan, Mrs. Pugh-
(Pronunciation)	Me fith ich kegin chee are dan, Mrs. Pugh.
(Translation)	Your kitchen will be on fire, Mrs. Pugh.
IDWAL:	'Nhad gai fynd i chwara yn nghae John Davies-
(Pronunciation)	Unhaad, gi vind i chwara in n'high, John Davies?
(Translation)	Father, may I go to play in John Davies' field?
A FATHER:	Ddim heddyw-dwisho ti garte-
(Pronunciation)	Thim hethu-dwisho tea-gartre.
(Translation)	No today—I need you at home.
1ST GIRL:	Yforty d'wi am drio sgwennu llythyr—
(Pronunciation)	E forty, dwee, am drio sgenny lhitheer.
(Translation)	I am going to try to write a letter.
2ND GIRL:	Os gynnachi steel-pen golew?
(Pronunciation)	Os ginnachy steel-pen goloo?
(Translation)	Do you have a fairly good steel pen?
WILL HUGHES:	Mae'na gymaint o flots!
(Pronunciation)	Minah giment o vlots.
(Translation)	There are so many blots.
3RD GIRL:	Dwi wedi sgwennu llythyr at fy nain, wni ddim be ddidi'thi.
(Pronunciation)	Dwee wedee s'gwenny lhitheer at ve nine ooni thim bey thidee thee.
(Translation)	I wrote a letter to my grandmother. I do not know what she will say.
WILL HUGHES:	Welsochi 'rioed eiriau fel one?
(Pronunciation)	Welso chee reeoid irrey vell een?
(Translation)	Did you ever see words like that?
SARA PUGH:	Fedri'thi ddim canu fel Cymraes, digon siwr-
(Pronunciation)	Vedree three thim Canee vell Kimrys diggon sure.
(Translation)	They cannot sing like the Welsh that's sure.
ROBBART ROBBATCH:	Mae'r hen ddyn am ofyn rwbeth iddi eto-drychwch arno-
(Pronunciation)	Myer hen theen am ovin rew beth ithi etto—droochuch arno.
(Translation)	The old man is going to ask something again, look at him.
SARAH PUGH:	Mi gollith'o ei Gymraeg cyn bo hir-
(Pronunciation)	My gollchith eye Kimraeg bo heer.
(Translation)	He will lose his welsh before long.
3RD GIRL:	Mae genni just ddigon o amswer i gyrraedd at y llyn—Mae'r dwr yn rhy oer i ymdrochi.
(Pronunciation)	My gennee just thigon o amswer e geeraeth at u llin. Myer doour unree oir u imdrochee.

| (Translation) | I have just enough time to reach the lake ——— |
| | The water is too cold to go bathing. |

ACT III

ROBBART:	Tyd, Idwal, mae o'n cysgu.
(Pronunciation)	Tid, Idwal, my o un kiskee.
(Translation)	Come, Idwal, he is sleeping.
	Tyd, Idwal
	Tid, Idwal
	Come, Idwal
	Tiddana, N'had
	Tidona, Unhaad
	Come away, Father.

PRONUNCIATION OF PROPER NAMES

(NOTE: The letter o is generally pronounced as in open and not as in on. The letter r is rolled, and s is hissed and never z.)

John Goronwy Jones	Jon Guronwee Jos
Miss Ronberry	Miss RONberry
Idwal Morris	IDwal MoRRis
Sarah Pugh	SARah Pugh
Mrs. Watty	Mrs. WaTTee
Bessie Watty	BESSie WaTTee
Miss Moffat	Miss MoFFat
Robbart Robbatch	RoBBart RoBBatch
Morgan Evans	MoRRgan EVans
Glyn Thomas	Glin Tomas
John Owen	Jon Oowan
Will Hughes	Will Hughes
Old Tom	Old Tom

7

The Corn Is Green, produced by Herman Shumlin, opened at the National Theater, New York, on November 26, 1940, with the following cast:

JOHN GORONWY JONES	Rhys Williams
MISS RONBERRY	Mildred Dunnock
IDWAL MORRIS	Charles S. Pursell
SARAH PUGH	Gwyneth Hughes
A GROOM	George Bleasdale
THE SQUIRE	Edmond Breon
MRS. WATTY	Rosalind Ivan
BESSIE WATTY	Thelma Schnee
MISS MOFFAT	Ethel Barrymore
ROBBART ROBBATCH	Thomas Lyons
MORGAN EVANS	Richard Waring
GLYN THOMAS	Kenneth Clarke
JOHN OWEN	Merritt O'Duel
WILL HUGHES	Terrence Morgan
OLD TOM	Sayre Crawley

BOYS, GIRLS and PARENTS: Julia Knox, Amelia Romano, Betty Conibear, Rosalind Carter, Harda Normann, Joseph McInerney, Marcel Dill, Gwilym Williams, Tommy Dix.

SYNOPSIS OF SCENES

ACT I

Scene 1—An afternoon in June.
Scene 2—A night in August, six weeks later.

ACT II

Scene 1—An early evening in August, two years later.
Scene 2—A morning in November, three months later.

ACT III

An afternoon in July, seven months later.

The action of the play takes place in the living room of a house in Glansarno, a small village in a remote Welsh countryside.

The time is the latter part of the last century, and covers a period of three years.

THE CORN IS GREEN

ACT I

SCENE 1: *The living room of a house in Glansarno, a small village in a remote Welsh countryside. A sunny afternoon in June, in the latter part of the last century. The house is old, and the ceiling slants away from the audience. Facing the audience, on the left [stage R.], narrow stairs lead up to a landing and then on the L. to a passage to the bedrooms, we can just see, facing, the door of one bedroom which is later to be Miss Moffat's. A door L. 2 leads to the kitchen, at the foot of the stairs an alcove and a door lead to a little room which is later the study. In the back wall, to R., the front door, with outside it a small stone porch faintly overgrown with ivy, and opening to the L. on to a path, in the back wall, to the L., a large bay window with a small sofa seat. In R. wall, downstage, the garden door, with above it a small side window, when the door is open we can just see a trellised porch with a creeper. · Through the thickish curtains over the bay window we glimpse a jagged stone wall and the sky.*

The floor is of stone flags, with one rug in front of the sofa. Faded sprigged wall-paper.

The furniture is a curious jumble of old Welsh and Victorian pieces. A large serviceable flat-topped desk under the side window, a desk-chair in front of it, a table with a small chair near the middle of the room, an armchair between the desk and the table, a sofa, down-stage, between the table and the foot of the stairs, in the back wall, near the kitchen door, an old Welsh dresser with plates and crockery, in the L. wall, against the staircase, a settle, in the window recess, a small table. In the back wall, to R. of the front door, a small grandfather's clock. An oil lamp on C. table, another on the desk. Another on the dresser.

The most distinctive feature of the room is the amount

9

*of books on the walls, of all sorts and sizes, some in
open bookcases, others on newly-built shelves, on practically every available space.
The kitchen door is open, there are books on the window seat.
As the curtain rises* MR. JOHN GORONWY JONES *and*
MISS RONBERRY *are arranging the last books in their
places, she is sitting on a tiny stool taking books out of
a large packing case and fitting them on to narrow
shelves between the garden door and the side window,
flicking each one mechanically with a tiny lace handkerchief. She is a gentlewoman in her thirties, with the
sort of pinched prettiness that tends to look sharp before
that age, especially when it makes sporadic attempts at
coquetry, she wears a hat. He is a shabby Welshman of
forty, bespectacled, gloomy and intense, a volcano,
harmless even in full eruption. He is perched on top of
a step-ladder, arranging books on a high shelf between
the front door and the bay window, dusting them vig-
orously before putting them in place.*

JONES. (*Singing in Welsh.*) ". . . Pechudur wyf, y dua'n fyw."
(*Etc.*)

(MISS RONBERRY *looks.*)

MISS RONBERRY. (*Seated on stool* R.) Your voice has given me an
agonizing headache. And if you must indulge in music—(*Puts
books in case.*)—will you please not do it in Welsh?
JONES. I wasn't indulgin' in music, I was sing'n' a hymn. (*Slight
pause.*) And if a hymn gives you a headache, there is nothing
wrong with the hymn; there is something wrong with your head.
(*Comes down.*)
MISS RON. I still don't see the necessity for it.
JONES. I sing to cheer myself up. (*Taking packing case, crosses
L.*)
MISS RON. What do the words mean?
JONES. "The wicked shall burn in hell." (*Exits into kitchen.*
MISS RON. *picks up packing case, starts up* L. IDWAL MORRIS *comes
in from garden, stops at door.*)
MISS RON. Oh! (*He is a thin, ragged boy of thirteen, very timid.
Up* R. C.) Is the garden nice and ready?

10

IDWAL. 'Sgwelwchi'n dda, d'wi'di torri'r bloda.

MISS RON. Translation! (*Crosses with box to chair up* L. *of arch in bay window—then to* L. *of* C. *table.*)

(JONES *returns from kitchen, crosses to below* R. *end of* C. *table.*)

IDWAL. (*Crosses in up* R. C.) Os gwelwchi'n dda, Mistar Jones, d'wi'di torri'r bloda, a mae'r domen yn hogla'n ofnadwy. (MISS RON. *crosses to him and takes flowers.*)

JONES. He says he cut the sweet peas and the rubbish-heap is smelling terrible.

MISS RON. (*Crosses up to small table.*) Oh dear. His father must put something on it. (*Arranges flowers in vase.*)

JONES. (*Going up ladder.*) That's the English all over. The devil is there, is he? Don't take him away, put a bit of scent on him! Gofyn i dy dad i roi rwbeth arno am heddyw. (MISS RON. L. *of* C. *table.*)

IDWAL. Diolch, syr. (*He runs off into garden again.*)

MISS RON. I hope he will have the sense to give the message.

JONES. (*Still on ladder.*) It is terrible, isn't it, the people on these green fields and flowery hillsides bein' turned out of Heaven because they cannot answer Saint Peter when he asks them who they are in English? It is wicked, isn't it, the Welsh children not bein' *born* knowing English—(MISS RON. *crosses* R. *to bookcase again.*)—isn't it? Good heavens, God bless my soul, by Jove, this that and the other!

MISS RON. Anybody in Wales will tell you that the people in this part of the countryside are practically barbarians. (SARAH PUGH *comes out of bedroom and down stairs. She is a buxom peasant-woman, with a strong Welsh accent.*) Not a single caller for fifteen miles, and even then ——

SARAH. (*Crosses to* C.) Please, miss—(MISS RON. *crosses* L. *a step.*)—I made the bed lovely. And I dust ——

MISS RON. That will be all, dear, the Colonel is bound to have his own man-servant. (*Picks up stool, crosses* L. *with it, places it below settle.*)

SARAH. (*Crosses up to* R. C. *door.*) Then I better have another sit down in my post office.

JONES. What is the matter with your post office?

SARAH. It has—(*Opens door.*)—not had a letter for seven weeks. Nobody but me can write, and no good *me* writin', because nobody but me can read. (JONES *crosses back of table.*) If I get a

11

telegram I put him in the window and I die straight off. (*She goes out, closes door.*)

MISS RON. You see? (*Crosses up, gets flowers from table in alcove, places them on* C. *table.*) I can't think why a Colonel should elect to come and live in this place. (*Patting flower into position.* L. *of* L. C. *table.*) There . . . I have never *seen* so many books! (JONES *up ladder.*) I do hope the—(*Crosses up.*)—curtains will not be too feminine. I chose them with such care —— (*Crosses down back of couch.*)

JONES. Why are you taking so much trouble getting somebody else's house ready for them?

MISS RON. (*Examines cushion.*) You need not have helped me if you did not wish! (*Crosses to settle for needle and thread.*) I am frightened of the spinning-wheel, too, and the china; his own furniture is *so* distinctive. The desk. And the waste-paper basket . . . So . . . so virile. (*Sits couch.*)

JONES. (*On ladder.*) Are you hoping that the Colonel will live up to his waste-paper basket?

MISS RON. That is horrid.

JONES. And then you will have two on a string: him and the Squire ——

MISS RON. Mr. Jones ——!

JONES. And if I was a bit more of a masher, there would be three. Worldly things, that is your trouble. " Please, Mistar Jones, my life is as empty as a rotten nutshell, so get me a husband before it is too late, double quick! " (*A knock at front door, it opens and a liveried* GROOM *appears.*)

MISS RON. You insulting man ——

GROOM. The Squire.

(*The* SQUIRE *follows him in. He is a handsome English country gentleman in his forties, wearing knickerbockers and gaiters, a hard drinker, bluff, kind, immensely vain, and, when the time comes, obtusely obstinate. The* GROOM *goes out again and shuts door.*)

MISS RON. (*Rises*) Squire . . .

SQUIRE. (*Crosses to her at* L.) Delicious lady, delicious surprise, and a merry afternoon to ye, as our forbears put it. . . . (*Hat on table* L. C.) How are you, Jones, making the most of your half-day?

JONES. (*Rises, on ladder.*) Good afternoon, sir ——

SQUIRE. Squat—(*Crosses to armchair* R. C.)—dear fellow, squat—
(MISS RON. *sits on couch.*)—no ceremony with me! . . . (*Places armchair* R. C., *sits.*) And why, dear lady, were you not at the Travers-Ellis wedding? (JONES *starts down with ladder.*)
MISS RON. Naughty! I sat next to you at the breakfast.
SQUIRE. By Jingo! So you did!
JONES. Excuse me —— (*Crosses down between them to* L. 1. *He goes into study.*)
SQUIRE. Deuced fine breakfast . . .
MISS RON. We had a talk about children.
SQUIRE. Did we? . . . Well, the next wedding we're at, there'll be *no* chance of my forgettin' you, eh?
MISS RON. Why?
SQUIRE. Because—(*Rises, crosses* R. *of armchair.*)—you'll be the stunning, blushing bride!
MISS RON. And who—will be the ——?
SQUIRE. Now that's what J want to know, because J'm going to give you away!
MISS RON. Oh! (JONES *returns from study, stops at* L. 1.)
SQUIRE. (*Crosses to table* C.) Now who's it going to be?
MISS RON. Squire, you are too impatient! I am taking my time!

(JONES *crosses up, places chair up, then to window seat—sits—dusts books.*)

SQUIRE. Too bad . . . (*Looks about room, crosses* L. *of armchair.*) No sign of the new inhabitant?
MISS RON. Any moment now, I think! The pony and trap met the London train at a quarter to twelve!
SQUIRE. Hasn't the fellow got his own private conveyance?
MISS RON. I think not.
SQUIRE. I hope he's all right.
MISS RON. He wrote very civilly to Mr. Jones about the house ——
SQUIRE. Oh, yes. Not a club, I remember, but the paper—not bad texture. (*Sits armchair* R. C.) Funny sort of chap, though, eh?
MISS RON. Why?
SQUIRE. All these books. (*A timid knock at front door up* R. IDWAL *enters, very frightened, stands two steps below door.*)
IDWAL. Os gwelwchi'n dda, syr, mae Mistar Tomos wedi 'ngyrru i yma ich gweld chi!
SQUIRE. (*Turns.*) Y'know, it's as bad as being abroad . . . been among it half my life, and never get used to it. (*Leans forward.*)

JONES. (*Comes down* R. *of table.*) The groom told him, sir, that you wanted to see him.

SQUIRE. Oh, yes—well, come here where I can see you, eh? . . . (IDWAL *crosses down* R. *of him,* SQUIRE *turns to him.*) Now, boy, how old are you—(*To* JONES.)—or whatever the Chinese is for it?

JONES. Just turned thirteen, sir.

SQUIRE. Thirteen? Well, why aren't you working in the mine over in the next valley? Don't like to see young fellows wasting their time, y'know.

JONES. He has got one lung funny.

SQUIRE. Oh, I see. . . . Rough luck—here, laddy, there's a six-pence for you, and remember all work and no play makes Taffy a dull boy!

IDWAL. Diolch yn faw, syr —— (*He runs out by front door.*)

SQUIRE. And tell your uncle I want Ranger shod ——

IDWAL. Diolch, syr ——

SQUIRE. And a gate mended ——

IDWAL. Diolch yn faw, syr —— (*He runs out by front door.*)

MISS RON. But he hasn't understood your orders!

SQUIRE. Neither he has ——

JONES. He thought the Squire was havin' a chat. I will tell his uncle ——

IDWAL. Tomos—Aneurin—dyma'r corbyd—(JONES *looks out window.*)—dewch i wel'd—fe ddwe-dai wrth y Scweiar—brysiwch!

MISS RON. (*Rises.*) That must be something —— (IDWAL *appears at front door, panting with expectation.*)

IDWAL. Pliss, syr, dyma'r carbyd! (*He darts back, leaving door open.*)

MISS RON. (*Crosses up* L. C., *looks out window.*) He must mean the Colonel—how gratifying ——

(BESSIE WATTY *wanders shyly in* R. *of door. She is an extremely pretty, plump little girl of fourteen, it is a moment before one realizes that her demureness is too good to be true. She wears her hair over her shoulders, is dressed very plainly, in a shabby sailor suit and hat, and carries brown-paper parcels. She is followed by* MRS. WATTY, *a middle-aged Cockney servant, dressed for travel-ing, carrying a hamper in her arms. Her self-confidence is not so*

14

overwhelming as the SQUIRE'S, *but it is quite as complete, and as kindly.*)

SQUIRE. Capital —— (*Crosses up* L. *of door.* MISS RON. *crosses down above couch,* L. *end.*)

MRS. WATTY. (*To* R. *of* SQUIRE. *To* SQUIRE.) D'you speak English?

SQUIRE. I do.

MRS. WATTY. Be a dear an' 'old this! (*Gives him hamper and exits front door.*)

SQUIRE. Crikey! A Colonel with an abigail! (*A step toward* BESSIE. *Catching* BESSIE'S *owl-like expression and stopping short.*) Why don't *you* say something?

BESSIE. I never speak till I'm spoken to.

SQUIRE. Oh . . . Well, who was that?

BESSIE. My Mummy. (*To* MISS RON.) I never had no daddy.

(MRS. WATTY *returns, with two large parcels, crosses to table* C.)

MRS. WATTY. My Gawd—(*Pause.*)—they're heavy. (*Puts parcels on table.*)

MISS RON. What are they? (*Crosses* R. MRS. WATTY.)

MRS. WATTY. Books. (*Takes hamper from* SQUIRE, *crosses to below desk.*)

SQUIRE. (*A step to* L. *of her.*) Is your employer with you, my good woman? (*Crosses to* R. *of* C. *table.*)

MRS. WATTY. No, followed be'ind, most of the way. Ought to be 'ere by now, I'll 'ave a see . . . (*Crosses up to door.*) 'Ere we are! Tally-o! (SQUIRE *crosses to couch* L.) Thought we'd lost you!

(*A pause.* MISS MOFFAT *comes in from road, wheeling a bicycle. She is about forty, a healthy Englishwoman with an honest face, clear, beautiful eyes, a humorous mouth, a direct friendly manner, and unbounded vitality, which is prevented from tiring the spectator by its capacity for sudden silences and for listening. Her most prominent characteristic is her complete unsentimentality She wears a straw hat, collar and tie, and a dark unexaggerated skirt, a satchel hangs from her shoulder* JONES *rises.*)

MISS MOFFAT. I was hoping to pass you, but that last hill was too much for me. Good afternoon.

ALL. Good afternoon.

MISS MOFFAT. There's a smallish crowd already, so I thought I'd

15

better bring Priscilla inside. Watty, can you find somewhere for her? (MISS MOFFAT *looks out window.*)

MRS. WATTY. Dunno I'm sure.

MISS MOFFAT. I think I'll have a look at the garden first. (*She goes out into garden.* SQUIRE *crosses to* R. 1. *Looks off.*)

MRS. WATTY. (*Wheeling bicycle gingerly towards kitchen.*) That must be my kitchen in there; we'll 'ave to 'ang 'er with the bacon. (*To* BESSIE.) Come on, girl, give us a 'and—(BESSIE *crossing* L.)—don't stand there gettin' into mischief!

BESSIE. I'm frightened of it.

MRS. WATTY. It won't bite you! Most it can do is catch fire, and I'll 'ave a drop o' water ready for it. (*Her voice fades away into kitchen.*)

BESSIE. (*At* L. *of* L. C. *table.*) Has anybody got a sweetie?

MISS RON. No.

BESSIE. Oh . . . (*She trails after* MRS. WATTY *into kitchen.* MISS MOFFAT *returns, crosses to* R. C.)

MISS MOFFAT. It's bigger than I expected. . . . (*Closes door.*) There! (*Puts satchel on desk.*) Good afternoon! So this is my house. . . .

SQUIRE. No, it isn't!

MISS MOFFAT. Oh? Isn't this Pengarth? (*Crosses in to* R.) The name of the building, I mean?

MISS RON. Yes, it is —— (MRS. WATTY *returns from kitchen, motions to* JONES *to unpack books in hamper, and takes kettle and its appurtenances back into kitchen.*)

MISS MOFFAT. That's right, it was left me by my uncle, Dr. Moffat. I'm Miss Moffat. (*Crosses to front of couch.*) ? take it you're Miss Ronberry, who so kindly corresponded with me?

SQUIRE. But sure—(*To* R. *of* MISS MOFFAT.)—those letters were written by a man?

MISS MOFFAT. Well, if they were I have been grossly deceiving myself for over thirty years. . . . Now this is jolly interesting. Why did it never occur to you that I might be a woman?

SQUIRE. Well—the paper wasn't scented ——

MISS RON. And such a bold hand —— (*Crosses down to* L. *below couch.*)

SQUIRE. And that long piece about the lease being ninety-nine years, don't you know ——

MISS MOFFAT. Was there anything wrong with it?

SQUIRE. No, there wasn't, that's the point.

16

MISS MOFFAT. I see.

MISS RON. And surely you signed your name very oddly?

MISS MOFFAT. My initials, L. C. Moffat? You see, I've never felt that Lily Christabel really suited me. (*Crosses to* R. *of armchair via above it.*)

MISS RON. And I thought—(*Sits couch.*)—it meant Lieutenant-Colonel. . . . But there *was* a military title after it!

MISS MOFFAT. (*At desk.*) M.A., Master of Arts.

SQUIRE. Arts? D'ye mean the degree my father bought me when I came down from the Varsity?

MISS MOFFAT. The very same. Except that I was at Aberdeen, and had to work jolly hard for mine. (*To below desk.*)

SQUIRE. (*Crosses to* R. C., L. *of her.*) A female M.A.? And how long's that going to last?

MISS MOFFAT. Quite a long time, I hope, considering we've been waiting for it for two thousand years. (*Crosses up to* JONES.)

JONES. Are you saved?

MISS MOFFAT. I beg your pardon? (*A step back.*)

JONES. Are you Church or Chapel?

MISS MOFFAT. I really don't know. . . . And now you know all about me, what do *you* do? (*Crosses to above table,* JONES *goes down* R.)

SQUIRE. I'm afraid I don't do anything. (*Crosses, takes hat from table, crosses to door up* R.)

MISS RON. Mr. Treverby owns the Hall!

MISS MOFFAT. (*Crosses to* SQUIRE.) Really. I've never had much to do with the landed gentry. Interesting.

SQUIRE. (*A step downstage.*) Au revoir, dear lady. 'Day, Jones. (*He goes frigidly out by front door.* JONES *closes door.*)

MISS MOFFAT. Well, nobody could say that I've made a conquest there. . . . What's the matter with him? (*Crosses to* L. 1, *study door.* MRS. WATTY *comes in from kitchen with tray and 3 cups, sugar bowl, creamer, spoons, to back of table* C.)

MRS. WATTY. I found the tea, ma'am; it *looks* all right ——

MISS MOFFAT. Good ——

MRS. WATTY. An' the big luggage is comin' after ——

MISS MOFFAT. (*At study door.*) This isn't a bad little room ——

MRS. WATTY. Where's his lordship?

MISS MOFFAT. (*Going upstairs.*) Took offence and left. (*She disappears down passage.*)

MRS. WATTY. (*Looks at them both.*) Took offence? At 'er?

MISS RON. I am afraid so. (MRS. WATTY *crosses to below desk, gets hamper.*)

MRS. WATTY. I'm jiggered! What d'you think of 'er, eh? Ain't she a clinker? (*To back of* C. *table.*)

MISS RON. She is unusual, is she not?

MRS. WATTY. She's a clinker, that's what. Terrible strong-willed, o' course, terrible. Get 'er into mischief, I keep tellin' 'er. Would bring me 'ere. I said no, I said, not with my past, I said.

MISS RON. Your past?

MRS. WATTY. Before she took me up. (*To* R. *of* L. C. *table.*) But what with 'er, and now I've joined the Corpse, it's all blotted out.

JONES. (*To* R. *of her.*) The Corpse?

MRS. WATTY. (*To* L. *of him.*) The Militant Righteous Corpse. Ran into 'em in the street I did, singin' and prayin' and collectin', full blast; and I been a different woman since. Are *you* saved?

JONES. Yes, I am.

MRS. WATTY. So'm I, ain't it lovely? (*Jones crosses* R.)

MISS RON. But what *was* . . . your past?

MRS. WATTY. Light fingers. (*Crosses to* R. *of table, front of it.*)

MISS RON. Light fingers? You mean—stealing?

MRS. WATTY. Everywhere I went. (*A step toward* MISS RON.) Terrible. Pennies, stockings, brooches, spoons, tiddly, anything. Every time there was a do, everything went; and I always knew it was me! (MISS MOFFAT *comes downstairs.*) I was just tellin' 'em about my trouble.

MISS MOFFAT. Well, don't tell them any more. (*Song off-stage.*) Is your kitchen all right?

MRS. WATTY. I ain't *seed* no mice yet. (*She goes into kitchen, takes hamper with her.*)

MISS MOFFAT. (*Crosses to* R. C.) I agree with the last tenant's taste. . . . You have arranged my things quite splendidly, Miss Ronberry, I do thank you—both of you. . . . (JONES *crosses up to small table.* MISS RON. *rises.*) I like this house. . . . What's that singing?

JONES. Boys coming home from the mine.

MISS RON. They burst into song on the slightest provocation. You mustn't take any notice —— (*Crosses* L. *a step.*)

MISS MOFFAT. I like it. . . . (*Crosses to window* R.) And those mountains. That grand wild countryside . . . the foreign-looking people . . . But business . . . I've heard about that mine. How far is it? (*Crosses* C. *upstage.*)

JONES. (*Points* L., *comes in.*) It is the Glasynglo coal mine, six miles over the hills.

MISS MOFFAT. Hm . . . (*Looks* L.)

MISS RON. We're hoping it will stay the only one, or our scenery will be ruined—such a pretty landscape ——

MISS MOFFAT. What is the large empty building next door?

JONES. Next door? The old barn belongin' to the Gwalia Farm, before the farm was burnt down —— (*Song fades out.*)

MISS MOFFAT. So it's free?

JONES. Free? Yes —— (*Crosses in to* R. C., R. *of* L. C. *table.*)

MISS RON. (*Rises.*) I am over-staying my welcome—so very charming ——

JONES. I also—all the volumes are dusted —— (*Starts to go toward her.*)

MISS MOFFAT. (*Crosses front of couch.*) I want you two people. Very specially. First you, Miss Ronberry. (*Sits couch.*) I used to meet friends of yours at lectures in London. You live alone, you have just enough money, you're not badly educated, and time lies heavy on your hands.

MISS RON. The Wingroves! (*Sits couch.*) How mean—I should never have thought ——

MISS MOFFAT. Isn't that so?

MISS RON. Not at all. When the right gentleman appears ——

MISS MOFFAT. If you're a spinster well on in her thirties, he's lost his way and isn't coming. Why don't you face the fact and enjoy yourself, the same as I do?

MISS RON. But when did you give up hope—oh, what a horrid expression ——

MISS MOFFAT. I can't recall ever having any hope. Visitors used to take a long look at my figure and say: " *She's* going to be the clever one."

MISS RON. But a woman's only future is to marry and—and fulfil the duties of ——

MISS MOFFAT. Skittles! I'd have made a shocking wife, anyway.

MISS RON. But haven't you ever—been in love?

MISS MOFFAT. No.

MISS RON. How very odd.

MISS MOFFAT. (JONES *turns.*) I've never talked to a man for more than five minutes without wanting to box his ears.

MISS RON. But how have you passed your time since ——?

19

MISS MOFFAT. Since I had no hope? Very busily. In the East End, for years.

MISS RON. Social service?

MISS MOFFAT. If you like; though there's nothing very social about washing invalids with every unmentionable ailment under the sun . . . I've read a lot, too. I'm afraid I'm what is known as an educated woman. Which brings me to Mr. Jones; the Wingroves told me all about you.

JONES. (*Crosses in to* R. C.) My conscience is as clear as the snow.

MISS MOFFAT. I'm sure it is, but you're a disappointed man, aren't you?

JONES. (*To* R. *of armchair.*) How can I be disappointed when I am saved?

MISS MOFFAT. Oh, but you can! You can't really enjoy sitting all by yourself on a raft, on a sea containing everybody you know. You're disappointed because you're between two stools.

JONES. Between two stools? On a raft?

MISS MOFFAT. Exactly. Your father was a grocer with just enough money to send you to a grammar-school, with the result that you are educated beyond your sphere, and yet fail to qualify for the upper classes. You feel frustrated, and fall back on being saved. Am I right?

JONES. It is such a terrible thing you have said that I will have to think it over. (*A step* R.)

MISS MOFFAT. Do —— (*Rises.*) But in the meantime—(*Pause.*) —would you two like to stop moping and be very useful to me?

MISS RON. Useful?

MISS MOFFAT. Yes, tell me—(*Crosses upstage.*)—within a radius of five miles, how many families are there round here?

MISS RON. Families? There's the Squire, of course, and Mrs. Gwent-Price in the little Plas Lodge, quite a dear thing ——

MISS MOFFAT. I mean ordinary people. (*Down to below and* R. *of table* L. C.)

MISS RON. The villagers?

MISS MOFFAT. Yes. How many families?

MISS RON. I really haven't the faint ——

JONES. (*Up to* R. *of* MISS MOFFAT.) There are about twenty families in the village and fifteen in the farms around.

MISS MOFFAT. Many children?

JONES. **What age?**

MISS MOFFAT. Up to sixteen or seventeen.

JONES. Round here they are only children till they are twelve. Then they are sent away over the hills to the mine, and in one week they are old men.

MISS MOFFAT. I see —— (*Crosses up* C.) How many can read or write?

JONES. Next to none. (*Crosses up to her.*)

MISS RON. Why do you ask?

MISS MOFFAT. (*At above desk chair.*) Because I am going to start a school for them.

MISS RON. Start a school for them? What for?

MISS MOFFAT. What for? (*Crosses to* R. *of* L. C. *table.*) See these books? Hundreds of 'em, and something wonderful to read in every single one—these nippers are to be cut off from all that, for ever, are they? Why? Because they happen to be born penniless in an uncivilized countryside, coining gold down there in that stinking dungeon for some beef-headed old miser!

JONES. That's right. . . . (*Follows her.*)

MISS MOFFAT. The printed page, what is it? One of the miracles of all time, that's what! And yet when these poor babbies set eyes on it, they might just as well have been struck by the miracle of sudden blindness; and that, to my mind, is plain infamous!

JONES. My goodness, Miss, that's right. . . .

MISS RON. The *ordinary* children, you mean?

MISS MOFFAT. Yes, my dear, the ordinary children, that came into the world by the same process exactly as you and I. When I heard that this part of the world was a disgrace to a Christian country, I knew this house was a godsend; I am going to start a school, immediately, next door in the barn, and you are going to help me! (*Crosses to* MISS RON.)

MISS RON. I? (*Rises.*)

MISS MOFFAT. Yes, you! You're going to fling away your parasol and your kid gloves, and you're going to stain those tapering fingers with a little honest toil!

MISS RON. I couldn't teach those children, I couldn't! They—they smell!

MISS MOFFAT. If we'd never been taught to wash, so would we; we'll put 'em under the pump. . . . Mr. Jones—(*To him,* L. *of*

21

armchair.)—d'ye know what I'm going to do with that obstinate head of yours?

JONES. My head?

MISS MOFFAT. I'm going to crack it open with a skewer. And I'm going to excavate all those chunks of grammar-school knowledge, give 'em a quick dust, and put 'em to some use at last ——

JONES. I am a solicitor's clerk in Gwaenygam and I earn thirty-three shillings per week ——

MISS MOFFAT. I'll give you thirty-four—and your lunch.

MISS RON. (*Crosses to* MISS MOFFAT.) I have an enormous house to run, and the flowers to do ——

MISS MOFFAT. Shut it up except one room, and leave—(*Crosses to desk, gets papers from satchel.*)—the flowers to die a natural death—in their own beds. I've been left a little money and I know exactly what I am going to do with it ——

JONES. But those children are in the mine—earning money—how can they ——

MISS MOFFAT. I'll pay their parents—(*Crosses to* R. *of* MISS RON. C. *via above.*)—the few miserable pennies they get out of it. . . . And when I've finished with you, *you* won't have time to think about snapping up a husband, and *you* won't have time to be so pleased that you're saved! Well?

JONES. (*Crosses to front of armchair.*) I do not care if you are not chapel, I am with you.

MISS MOFFAT. Good! I have all the details worked out—(*Sits couch.*)—I'll explain roughly. . . . Come along—(*Pulls* MISS RON.—*flourishes papers.* MISS RON. *sits* R. *of her.* JONES *crosses, sits* L. *of her on couch.*)—my dears, gather round, children— gather round —— Of course, we must go slowly at first, but if we put our backs into it . . . Here we are, three stolid middle-aged folk, settled in our little groove and crammed with benefits; and there are those babbies scarcely out of the shell, that have no idea they are even breathing the air. . . . Only God can know how their life will end, but He will give us the chance to direct them a little of the way ——

JONES. We have the blessed opportunity to raise up the children from the bowels of the earth where the devil hath imprisoned them in the powers of darkness, and bring them to the light of knowledge ——

MRS. WATTY. (*Coming in from kitchen.*) Here's the tea!

MISS MOFFAT. Each of us can take several classes, not only for the children, but their fathers and their mothers, and the older people too.

(CURTAIN FALLS *and rises immediately on—*)

ACT I

SCENE 2: *A night in August, six weeks later. The window-curtains are closed and the lamps lit. The armchair has been pushed* R. *of table and two small benches, one up and downstage, the other facing the audience. Red geraniums in pots across window-sills.* MISS MOFFAT'S *straw hat is slung over knob at foot of stairs. The big desk, sofa and settle are littered with books, exercise books, and sheets of paper. Apart from these details the room is unchanged.*

Sitting on the bench are five black-faced MINERS, *between twelve and sixteen years of age, wearing caps, mufflers, boots and corduroys embedded in coal, they look as if they had been commanded to wait. They all look alike under their black, the ring-leader is* MORGAN EVANS, *fifteen, quick and impudent, his second is* ROB-BART ROBBATCH, *a big, slow boy, a year or two older, the others are* GLYN THOMAS, WILL HUGHES *and* JOHN OWEN. *They all hum at rise.*

MRS. WATTY *comes downstairs, carrying a basket of washing.*

MRS. WATTY. You 'ere again? (*On stairs, stops halfway down.*)
ROBBART. Be mai'n ddeud?
MRS. WATTY. I said, you 'ere again?
MORGAN. No, Miss.
MRS. WATTY. What d'ye mean, no, Miss?
MORGAN. We issn't 'ere again, Miss.
MRS. WATTY. What are you, then? (*Comes down to stage level.*)
MORGAN. We issn't the same lot ass this mornin', Miss.
MRS. WATTY. Ain't you?
MORGAN. Miss Ronny-berry tell us to wait, Miss.
MRS. WATTY. Ma'am! (*Crossing up to kitchen door.*)

23

MISS MOFFAT. (*In bedroom.*) Yes?

MRS. WATTY. Five more nigger-boys for you! (*She goes into kitchen.* BOYS *bum again. Rum bottle business*—MORGAN. JONES *comes in from front door, crosses to back of* L. C. *table.*)

MORGAN. Sh! Good evenin', sir. (*Crosses to* R. *of* JONES.)

JONES. Good evening. (*Tips hat—back* L. *a step.*)

MORGAN. (*Crosses to* R. *of* L. C. *table.*) I seed you and the lady teacher be'ind the door! (*A laugh from him and others.*)

JONES. You wait till you see Miss Moffat. She will give you what for.

MORGAN. (*Shaking finger at* BOYS.) You wait till you see Miss Moffat. She will give you what for! (JONES *goes into kitchen.* ROBBART *repeats:* "*You wait till you see Miss Moffat, she will give you what for!*") Shh! (MISS MOFFAT *comes downstairs from bedroom.*)

MISS MOFFAT. I told you the shape of the bedroom doesn't allow for a door into the barn—oh, she isn't here. . . . (*Crosses* C.) Sorry to keep you waiting, boys, but I have to go across to Mr. Rees, the carpenter, and then I'll be able to talk to you. In the meantime, will you go to the pump in the garden shed, and wash your hands. Through there. You'll find a lantern. Did you understand all that? (*Starts up—stops.*)

MORGAN. Yes, Miss.

OTHERS. Thank you, Miss.

MISS MOFFAT. Good. (*Starts to go.*)

MORGAN. Please, Miss, can I have a kiss?

MISS MOFFAT. (*Returns.*) What did you say?

MORGAN. Please, Miss, can I have a kiss?

MISS MOFFAT. Of course you can. (*Puts her foot on bench—takes him by the neck and bends him over her knee and spanks him with the plan she carries.*) Can I oblige anybody else? (*She goes out by front door.* MORGAN *crosses up* C., *closes door.*)

ROBBART. Please, Miss, can I 'ave a smack bottom? (*All laugh.*)

WILL. Na-beth of Naw-stee.

MORGAN. Cythral uffarn ——

ROBBART. Nawn—(*Rises.*)—i drio molchi—dewch hogia—(*All rise—start off.*)—mae'n well nag eistedd yma—dewch ——

GLYN. Be hari hi—hi a'i molchi ——

JOHN. Pwy sisho molchi ——

WILL. Welso ti'rioed wraig fel ene ——

MORGAN. Mae'n lwcus na ddaru mi mo'i thrawo hi lawr a'i lladd hi ——

GLYN. Nog a senity Morgan back.

ROBBART. Comaranau corgee foal.

JOHN. Dinna auteb e-t.

WILL. Jobin dau de owl.

MORGAN. Ka da geg. (*They lumber off into the garden, close door.*)

(JONES' *head appears timidly from kitchen. He sees they are gone, gives a sigh of relief, and comes into room, carrying books, crosses, looks out window, sits desk and hums.* BESSIE *comes in from front door, crosses to table, puts hat on table. Sighs.*)

BESSIE. (*Crosses to* L. *of* JONES.) Would you like a sweetie? (*Opens bag.*)

JONES. No, thank you, my little dear. Have you had another walk?

BESSIE. (R. C.) Yes, Mr. Jones. All by myself.

JONES. Did you see anybody?

BESSIE. Only a lady and a gentleman in the lane—(JONES *turns to work.*)—and Mother told me never to look. . . . (JONES *looks at her.*) I do miss the shops. London's full o' them, you know.

JONES. Full of fancy rubbish, you mean.

BESSIE. I'd like to be always shopping, I would. Sundays and all. . . .

MRS. WATTY. Bessie!

BESSIE. Mr. Jones —— (*Crosses to* L. *of him.*) Is it true the school idea isn't going on that well?

JONES. Who told you that?

BESSIE. Miss Ronberry was sayin' something to my Mum—oh, I wasn't listenin'! . . . Besides, we've been here six weeks, and nothin's started yet.

JONES. Everything is splendid.

BESSIE. Oh, I am glad. (*Crosses to back of* L. C. *table.*) Miss Moffat's been cruel to me, but I don't bear no grudge.

JONES. Cruel to you?

BESSIE. She hides my sweets. (*Going.*) She's a liar, too. (*Starts* L., *returns.*)

JONES. A liar?

BESSIE. Told me they're bad for me —— (*Crosses to* R. *of table.*) And it says on the bag they're nourishin'. . . . And the idea of learnin' school with those children, ooh . . . (*Crosses* L. *to door.*)

JONES. Why are you holding your hair like that?

BESSIE. These are my curls. D'you think it's nice?

JONES. It is nice, but it is wrong.

MRS. WATTY. (*Calling shrilly, in kitchen.*) Bess-ie!

BESSIE. (*Starts* L.) I've been curlin' each one round me finger and holdin' it tight till it was all right. (*Stops.*) My finger's achin' something terrible. (*She goes into kitchen. A knock at front door.*)

JONES. Dewch ifewn. (IDWAL *appears with school bell. puts it down* R. *below couch, starts back up to* R. *door: Note—the bell is in a crate one foot square that opens on the side.* MISS RON. *comes in from study, sits settle at stair.*)

IDWAL. Cloch yr ysgol, Mistar Jones.

JONES. Diolch, ymachgeni. (*Pause.*) Nosdawch.

IDWAL. Nosdawch, Mistar Jones. (*He goes back through front door.*)

MISS RON. It says here that eight sevens are fifty-six. Then it says that seven eights are fifty-six—I can't see that at all. (MISS MOFFAT *returns from front door, crosses to back of* L. C. *table, puts down papers.*) Well?

MISS MOFFAT. No good.

MISS RON. Oh, dear.

MISS MOFFAT. Mr. Rees says he's had a strict order—(*Crosses down via* R. *of table to front of it.*)—not to discuss lining the roof till the lease of the barn is signed.

JONES. Who gave the order?

MISS MOFFAT. That's what I want to know.

MISS RON. And when will the lease be signed?

MISS MOFFAT. Never, it seems to me. Did you call at the solicitor's?

JONES. They have located Sir Herbert Vezey, but he is now doubtful about letting the barn and will give his decision by post.

MISS MOFFAT. But why? (JONES *turns away.*) He'd already said it was no use to him. And my references were impeccable. . . . *Why?* (*Sits couch.*)

MISS RON. You look tired.

MISS MOFFAT. It's been a bit of a day. A letter from the mine to say no child can be released above ground—that's all blethers, but still . . . A request from the public house not to start a school in case it interferes with beer-swilling and games of chance.

A message from the chapel people to the effect that I am a foreign adventuress with cloven feet; a bit of a day. (MRS. WATTY *comes in from kitchen, to* L. *end above table.*)

MRS. WATTY. Drop o' tea, ma'am, I expect you've 'ad a bit of a day. . . .

MISS MOFFAT. Who was that at the back, anything important?

MRS. WATTY. Only the person that does for that Mrs. Gwent-Price. Would you not 'ave your school opposite her lady because of her lady's 'eadaches.

MISS MOFFAT. What did you say?

MRS. WATTY. I pulverized 'er. I said it would be a shame, I said, if there was such a shindy over the way that the village couldn't hear Mrs. Double-Barrel givin' her 'usband what for, I said. (*Starts* L.) The person didn't know where to put 'erself. (*She goes back into kitchen.*)

JONES. That has not helped the peace in the community, neither.

MISS MOFFAT. I know, but she does make a tip-top cup of tea. . . . What's that?

JONES. It is the bell, for the school.

MISS MOFFAT. Oh, is it?

MISS RON. (*Rises.*) The bell? Do let us have a peep ——

JONES. (*Crosses to* R. C.) It was on Llantalon Monastery before it burnt down ——

MISS MOFFAT. Look, it's got the rope, and everything. . . . Well, it's good to see it, anyway.

MISS RON. (*At* L. *end of couch.*) The mason finished the little tower for it yesterday —— (*Crosses to* L. *of* JONES. *He backs* R.) Do let us tell those boys to put it up! It'll bring us luck!

MISS MOFFAT. If it keeps them out of mischief till I'm ready ——

MISS RON. (*Crosses to* JONES.) Mr. Jones, do go and tell them!

(JONES *backs again.* JONES *goes toward garden. As he opens door,* JOHN OWEN *shouts:* "Ah—Mr. Jones can do it." *All* BOYS *laugh.*)

MISS MOFFAT. Poor Jonesy, he's terrified of 'em.

MISS RON. So am I. They're so big. And so black —— (*Crosses up* L. SARAH *runs in, excited, leaving door open behind her.*)

SARAH. A letter from the gentleman that own the barn, I had a good look at the seal!

MISS MOFFAT. At last ——

MISS RON. What does it say? (*At up* C., R. *of table.*)

MISS MOFFAT. Sir Herbert still cannot give a definite decision until the seventeenth. Another week wasted. This is infuriating.

MISS RON. Does it mean he may not let you have it?

SARAH. Oh . . .

MISS MOFFAT. He must—it would ruin everything ——

MISS RON. Sarah—(*Crosses up* L. *of her.*)—isn't there another empty building *anywhere* round here?

SARAH. There is the pigstyes on the Maes Road, but they issn't big enough. (*She goes.*)

MISS RON. (*Crosses back of* L. C. *table.*) Oh, dear! Can't we start afresh somewhere else?

MISS MOFFAT. I've spent too much on preparations here—besides, I felt so right here from the start—I *can't* leave now . . . I'm a Christian woman, but I could smack Sir Herbert's face till my arm dropped off. (*Front door is opened unceremoniously and the* SQUIRE *strides in, he is in full evening dress.*)

SQUIRE. Jolly good evenin', teacher. Remember me? (MISS RON. *crosses down* L.)

MISS MOFFAT. Would you mind going outside, knocking, and waiting quite a long time before I say " Come in " ?

SQUIRE. Jolly good! Parlor games, what?

MISS RON. (*Crosses in a step.*) But, Miss Moffat, it's the *Squire!* Squire, you must forget you ever saw me in this dress—so ashamed —I shan't be a moment —— (*She runs upstairs into bedroom.*)

SQUIRE. Rat tat tat, one two three four come in, one two three four, forward *march!* My dear madam, you're not in class now! (*A knock at garden door.*) Come in! (ROBBART *and* MORGAN *enter from garden. Hats off.*)

ROBBART. Please, Miss, for the bell.

SQUIRE. 'Evening, boys! (*Enter* JONES.) 'Evening, Jones. I am appalled to observe, my boys, that you are still soiling your fingers in that disgusting coal-mine! (ROBBART *crosses to bell at couch.*)

JONES. Excuse me, please. . . . (*He goes into study* L. 1.)

SQUIRE. What's that you've got there?

ROBBART. Bell, syr, for the school.

SQUIRE. Up with it, boys, up with it! (ROBBART *lifts crate and carries it out garden door, which* MORGAN *has opened for him. MORGAN follows him, shutting door.*) Ding dong bell—teacher's in the well! . . . (*Crosses to couch.*) Now, my dear madam ——

MISS MOFFAT. I'm rather irritable this evening, so unless there's a reason for your visit ——

SQUIRE. (C.) Oh, but there is! Very important message. Word of mouth. From a gent that's just been dining with me. Sir Herbert Vezey.

MISS MOFFAT. Yes? . . . Oh, do be quick . . . !

SQUIRE. He has definitely decided that he has no use for the barn —but . . . (*Crosses to* R. *of armchair.*) . . . he does not see it as a school, and under no circumstances will he let it as such, so he must regretfully decline, et cetera. (*Crosses to front of armchair.*)

MISS MOFFAT. He implied in his first letter that he would be willing to sell.

SQUIRE. Then some big-wig must have made him change his mind, mustn't he?

MISS MOFFAT. You?

SQUIRE. (*Crosses to* R. *of couch.*) I have not called on you, madam, because I have been eyeing your activities very closely from afar—it is with dis-disapproval and—er—dis ——

MISS MOFFAT. It is unwise to embark on a speech with the vocabulary of a child of five.

SQUIRE. I am not going to have any of this damned hanky-panky in my village!

MISS MOFFAT. *Your* village!

SQUIRE. *My* village! I am no braggart, but I'd have you know that everything you can see from that window—(*Gestures* R. *window.*) —and you haven't got a bad view—*I* own! Now, my dear madam ——

MISS MOFFAT. And stop calling me your dear madam; I'm not married, I'm not French, and you haven't the slightest affection for me!

SQUIRE. (*Crosses to* R. C.) Oh . . . First of all, I'm not one to hit a woman below the belt. If you know what I mean. Always be fair—to the fair sex. . . . All my life I've done my level best for the villagers—they call me Squire, y'know, term of affection, jolly touching—I mean, a hamper every Christmas, the whole shoot, and a whopping tankard of beer on my birthday, and on my twenty-firster they all got a mug —— (*Crosses front of armchair.*)

MISS MOFFAT. Go on.

SQUIRE. They jabber away in that funny lingo, but bless their hearts, it's a free country! (*Crosses* L. C.) But puttin' 'em up to read English, and pothooks, and givin' 'em ideas—if there were more people like you, y'know, England'd be a jolly dangerous place to live in! What d'ye want to do, turn 'em into gentlemen? What's the idea? (*Crosses* R. C.)

MISS MOFFAT. I am beginning to wonder myself.

SQUIRE. Anyway, this buyin' 'em out of the mine is a lot of gammon. I own a half-share in it.

MISS MOFFAT. That explains a good deal.

SQUIRE. Why don't you take up croquet? Keep yourself out of mischief. (MISS RON. *comes out of bedroom.*) Well, dear lady, anything I can do to make your stay here a happier one —— (*Crosses* L.)

MISS MOFFAT. Thank you.

SQUIRE. I must be getting back. If I know Sir Herbert—(*Crosses to door.*)—my best old port will be no more ——

MISS MOFFAT. Wait a minute. (SQUIRE *comes down a step.*)

SQUIRE. Yes? (MISS MOFFAT *rises.*)

MISS MOFFAT. I know I shall be sticking a pin into a whale, but here are just two words about yourself. You are the Squire Bountiful, are you? Adored by his contented subjects, intelligent and benignly understanding, are you? I should just like to point out that there is a considerable amount of dirt, ignorance, misery and discontent abroad in this world, and that a good deal of it is due to people like you, because you are a stupid, conceited, greedy good-for-nothing—(*Up to him. Enter* MISS RON. *on landing.*) —addle-headed nincompoop, and you can go to blue blazes. (*Crosses him to down* R.) Good night!

SQUIRE. I perceive that you have been drinking. (*He goes.* MISS RON. *comes downstairs, crosses* R. C.)

MISS MOFFAT. That was undignified, but I feel better for it. (*Sits bench* R.)

MISS RON. I am glad—(*Crosses to* L. *of bench.*)—because it *was* plain-spoken, wasn't it? Has he been nasty? So unlike the Squire ——

MISS MOFFAT. He was kindness itself. He advised me to go and live in a hole in the ground with my knitting. He has persuaded the owner not to sell.

MISS RON. Oh, dear . . . of course . . . (*Sits* L. *of* MISS MOFFAT *on bench.*) . . . I always think men know best, don't you?

MISS MOFFAT. Yes.

MISS RON. I'm wearing my mousseline de soie, and he never even noticed . . . (MISS MOFFAT *crosses to* C.) . . . What will you do?

MISS MOFFAT. Sell the house; take this brain-child of a ridiculous spinster, and smother it. Have you got a handkerchief?

MISS RON. Yes, Miss Moffat. Why?

MISS MOFFAT. I want to blow my nose.

MISS RON. You ought to have had a cry. I love a cry when I'm depressed. (MISS MOFFAT *crosses to study* L. 1.) Such an advantage over the gentlemen, I always think ——

MISS MOFFAT. (*Calls off.*) Mr. Jones ——

JONES. (*Off* L.) Yes?

MISS MOFFAT. Will you write letters to the tradespeople and the mine? We are giving up the school. . . .

JONES. (*Off.*) Oh!

MISS MOFFAT. (*Crosses to desk* R., *gets tray with exercise books, crosses to couch* L.) I suppose we'd better start putting some order into this chaos, and get the business over. . . . What are these filthy exercise books doing among my papers? . . .

MISS RON. (*Rises to* L. *of desk.*) Those hooligans just now. They said Mr. Jones had picked them out because they could write English—(*Picks up books.*)—and would —— (*Crosses to table* C. *front of it.*) I mind my own some-dreadful-word business.

MISS MOFFAT. I set them an essay on " How I Would Spend My Holiday." I must have been mad. . . . (*Throws one book away and takes one from* MISS RON.)

MISS RON. (*Reading—laboriously.*) " If—I has ever holiday— (*Crosses to desk* R.)—I has breakfast and talks then dinner and a rest, tea then nothing—then supper then I talk and I go sleep."

MISS MOFFAT. From exhaustion, I suppose. (BESSIE *comes in from kitchen, crosses back of couch, gets hat from table and starts for door* U. R.) Where are you going?

BESSIE. Just another walk —— (*Sniffs.*) Miss Moffat. (*Crosses up* R.)

MISS RON. What's the matter, little dear?

BESSIE. Mum's hit me.

MISS RON. Oh, naughty mum. Why?

BESSIE. Just because I told her she was common. (*She goes out door up* R.)

MISS RON. That child is unhappy. (*Crosses to front of* L. C. *table.*)

MISS MOFFAT. I can't be bothered with her. Another time I'd have

31

been faintly amused by this one's idea of a holiday, judging by a rather crude drawing.

MISS RON. What is it?

MISS MOFFAT. A bicycling tour with me in bloomers.

MISS RON. Tch, tch . . . (*Crosses to settle at stairs.*)

MISS MOFFAT. " 'Holiday-time.' That carefree magic word! What shall it be this year, tobogganing among the eternal snows or tasting the joys of Father Neptune? "

MISS RON. But that's beautiful! Extraordinary!

MISS MOFFAT. I might think so too if I hadn't seen it in a book open on that desk. (*Throws book in waste-basket.*)

MISS RON. Oh!

MISS MOFFAT. No, your Squire was right . . . I have been a stupid and impractical ass, and I can't imagine how —— (*Looks at name on book. She begins to read, slowly, with difficulty.*) "The mine is dark. . . . If a light come in the mine . . . the rivers in the mine will run fast with the voice of many women; the walls will fall in, and it will be the end of the world." (MISS RON. *turns to* MISS MOFFAT. MORGAN *enters from garden door R. 1.* ROBBART *is with him, stays at door.*)

MORGAN. We put up the bell, Miss.

MISS RON. Shhh—the garden —— (ROBBART *exits,* MORGAN *starts, stops at door. To* MISS MOFFAT.) Do go on —— (MISS RON. *crosses to back of couch.*)

MISS MOFFAT. (*Reading.*) ". . . So the mine is dark . . ." (*Reading.*) ". . . But when I walk through the Tan—something —shaft, in the dark, I can touch with my hands the leaves on the trees, and underneath . . . where the corn is green." (*Looks at* MORGAN.)

MORGAN. Go on readin'.

MISS MOFFAT. (*Reading.*) ". . . There is a wind in the shaft, not carbon monoxide they talk about, it smell like the sea, only like as if the sea had fresh flowers lying about . . . and that is my holiday." (*Looks at name on book.* MORGAN *starts off—turns quickly as she speaks.*) Are you Morgan Evans?

MORGAN, Yes, Miss.

MISS MOFFAT. Did you write this?

MORGAN. No, Miss.

MISS MOFFAT. But it's in your book.

MORGAN. Yes, Miss.

MISS MOFFAT. Then who wrote it?

MORGAN. I dunno, Miss. (MISS MOFFAT *nods to* MISS RON., *who patters discreetly into study, closes door.*)

MISS MOFFAT. Did you write this?

MORGAN. I dunno, Miss . . . What iss the matter with it?

MISS MOFFAT. Sit down. (*He sits bench* R.) And take your cap off. (*He takes off his cap.*) Spelling's deplorable, of course. " Mine " with two " n's," and " leaves " l, e, f, s.

MORGAN. What was it by rights?

MISS MOFFAT. A " V," to start with.

MORGAN. I never 'eard o' no " v's," Miss.

MISS MOFFAT. Don't call me Miss.

MORGAN. Are you not a Miss?

MISS MOFFAT. Yes, I am, but it is not polite.

MORGAN. Oh.

MISS MOFFAT. You say, " Yes, Miss Moffat," or " No, Miss Moffat." M, o, double f, a, t.

MORGAN. No " v's " ?

MISS MOFFAT. No " v's." Where do you live?

MORGAN. Under the ground, Miss.

MISS MOFFAT. I mean your home.

MORGAN. Llyn-y-Mwyn, Miss . . . Moffat. Four miles from 'ere.

MISS MOFFAT. How big is it?

MORGAN. Four 'ouses and a beer-'ouse.

MISS MOFFAT. Have you any hobbies?

MORGAN. Oh, yes.

MISS MOFFAT. What?

MORGAN. Rum. (*Takes small bottle of rum out of pocket.*)

MISS MOFFAT. Rum? Do you live with your parents?

MORGAN. No, by my own self. My mother iss dead, and my father and my four big brothers wass in the Big Shaft Accident when I wass ten.

MISS MOFFAT. Killed?

MORGAN. Oh, yes, everybody wass.

MISS MOFFAT. What sort of man was your father?

MORGAN. 'E was a mongrel.

MISS MOFFAT. A what?

MORGAN. 'E had a dash of English. He learned it to me.

MISS MOFFAT. D'you go to chapel?

MORGAN. No, thank you.

MISS MOFFAT. Who taught you to read and write?

MORGAN. Tott?

MISS MOFFAT. Taught. The verb " to teach."

MORGAN. Oh, teached.

MISS MOFFAT. Who taught you?

MORGAN. I did.

MISS MOFFAT. Why?

MORGAN. I dunno.

MISS MOFFAT. What books have you read?

MORGAN. Books? A bit of the Bible and a book that a feller from the Plas kitchen nab for me.

MISS MOFFAT. What was it?

MORGAN. *The Ladies' Companion!* (MISS MOFFAT *rises, crosses up* R. C., *looks at him.* MORGAN *rises.*) Can I go now, pliss ——?

MISS MOFFAT. No. (MORGAN *sits.*) Do you want to learn any more?

MORGAN. No, thank you.

MISS MOFFAT. Why not?

MORGAN. The other men would have a good laugh.

MISS MOFFAT. (*Crosses back to armchair* R. *of table.*) I see. Have you ever written anything before this exercise?

MORGAN. No.

MISS MOFFAT. Why not?

MORGAN. Nobody never ask me to. What iss the matter with it?

MISS MOFFAT. (*Moves armchair* R. *of table.*) Nothing's the matter with it. (*Sits armchair,* R. *of table.*) Whether it means anything is too early for me to say, but it shows exceptional talent for a boy in your circumstances.

MORGAN. Terrible long words, Miss Moffat.

MISS MOFFAT. This shows that you are very clever.

MORGAN. Oh.

MISS MOFFAT. Have you ever been told that before?

MORGAN. It iss news to me.

MISS MOFFAT. What effect does the news have on you?

MORGAN. It iss a bit sudden. It makes me that I—I want to get more clever still. I want to know what iss—behind of all them books. . . .

MISS MOFFAT. (*Rises, crosses to* L. C.) Miss Ronberry . . . (*To him.*) Can you come tomorrow?

MORGAN. (*Rises.*) Tomorrow—no—I am workin' on the six till four shift ——

MISS MOFFAT. Then can you be here at five?

MORGAN. Five—no, not before seven, Miss—six miles to walk ——

MISS MOFFAT. Oh, yes, of course—seven, then. In the meantime I'll correct this for spelling and grammar. (*Crosses* L. *front of couch.*)

MORGAN. Yes, Miss Moffat.

MISS MOFFAT. That will be all. Good night.

MORGAN. Good night, Miss Moffat. (*Crosses to door up* R.)

MISS MOFFAT. Are you the one I spanked? (*He turns at door, looks at her, smiles, blinks and goes.*) Miss Ronberry! (*Crosses to* L. *then in to* R. *of* C.) Mr. Jones! (MISS RON. *runs in from study, as* MISS MOFFAT *is* C.)

MISS RON. Yes?

MISS MOFFAT. I have been a deuce of a fool. It doesn't matter about the barn; we are going to start the school—(*Crosses* C.) —in a small way at first, in this room. . . . And I am going to get those youngsters out of that mine if I have to black my face and go down and fetch them myself! Get Jonesy before he posts those letters, and tell those others I'll be ready for them in five minutes. (MISS RON. *starts to door* L. 1. MISS MOFFAT *crosses* L.) We are going on with the school! (*Crosses* C. MISS RON. *scampers into study. Her voice is heard, calling:* "*We are going on with the school!*" *Reading.*) ". . . and when I walk—in the dark . . . I can touch with my hands . . . where the corn is green. . . ." (*School bell rings—*)

MEDIUM CURTAIN

ACT II

SCENE 1: *The same. An early evening in August, two years later, the sun is still bright.*

The room is now a complete jumble of living-room and schoolroom, and there is every sign of cheerful over-crowding. The table in the window recess is replaced by double school desks, the table and its small chair are pushed behind sofa, a school desk stands isolated between the big open-top desk and sofa, between sofa and bay window, two rows of four school desks each, squeezed together and facing the audience at an angle. Charts, maps, an alphabet list are pinned up higgledy-piggledy over all the books, a large world globe on shelf, hat-pegs have been fixed irregularly back of R. door above and below kitchen door—1 peg above study door. Books overflow everywhere, all over the dresser especially, in place of plates, hat-pegs are loaded with caps and hats, cloak hangs on a hook on the back of the front door, a blackboard lies on sofa upside down, with " Constantinople is the capital of Turkey " written across in MISS RONBERRY'S tremulous handwriting. The lamp on the table has been removed. Potted plants on window-sills.

Before the CURTAIN RISES, VOICES are heard singing, in harmony, in Welsh, " Bugeilio'r Gwenyth Gwyn ", CHILDREN shrill, sweet and self-confident, reinforced by harmony from older boys and parents, especially SARAH.

The room seems full of people, MISS RONBERRY stands perched on the tiny stool between sofa and foot of stairs, her back to the audience, conducting stiffly, JONES is crouched in desk chair, correcting exercises at the open desk. SARAH, two older PEASANT WOMEN in shawls, and three older MEN in their shabby best stand crowded behind the eight desks and in the window recess. In front row of desks sit ROBBART, IDWAL, a little GIRL, and GLYN THOMAS; in second sit another little BOY, another little GIRL, BESSIE, and WILL HUGHES. In another desk pushed provisionally next front row sits

JOHN OWEN, *and in the other isolated one sits* OLD TOM, *an elderly, distinguished-looking peasant, has cap and stick before him, carried away by the music.*

BESSIE *is silent, bored, and prettier than ever, though still dressed as a sober little schoolgirl. The* BOYS *we saw before as miners are clean and almost spruce, the parents follow every movement of* MISS RONBERRY'S *with avid curiosity. The* PUPILS *have slates and slate pencils in front of them. The song is sung through to the end.*

MISS RON. Now that was quite better. Full of splendid feeling, and nice and precise as well. Have you all got my English translation? (*Steps down a step to them.*)

PUPILS. Yes, Miss Ronberry.

MISS RON. Are you all quite sure of the meaning of " Thou lovedest him, fair maid, that doth not love thee back? " (*Four* OLDER PEOPLE *follow with motion of lips.*)

PUPILS. Yes, Miss Ronberry. (FOUR PEOPLE *speak the line after* OTHERS *have said it.*)

OLD TOM. (*Singing stentoriously, in broken English.*) " That doth not luff thee . . . ba-a-ck! "

MISS RON. Capital, Mr. Tom. (*Crosses to table for bell.*) Home sweet home, children! (*Rings bell.*) Boys and girls, come out to play! (MISS PUGH *nudges* IDWAL.)

IDWAL. Please, Miss Ronberry, can we have some more?

MISS RON. Well, just the tiniest lesson. (*Replaces bell.*) We must keep to the curriculum. (*Steps up on stool again.*) Now what would you like?

IDWAL. Please, Miss Ronberry, how do you spell it?

MISS RON. What, dear?

OLD TOM. Curriculum. (*They murmur " Yes."*)

MISS RON. What would you like? The rivers of Europe or King Alfred and the cakes?

OLD TOM. Multiplication table! (*Some say " Yes." Others repeat multiplications.*)

MISS RON. Well, twice six are twelve! (*One old* MAN *does not recite. He smiles.*)

PUPILS. Twice seven are fourteen—twice eight are sixteen ——

OLD TOM. Twice thirteen are twenty-six!

MISS RON. Capital—school dismissed. (IDWAL *crosses front of desk to window* R. *All rise except* BESSIE.)

(*The following seven speeches spoken together.*)

37

CLARKE. Be'di'r gloch, Merry? (*Seated.*)
ROMANO. Chwarter i bump.

KNOX. What iss the next thing in the multiplication?
DIX. Wn i ddim yn wyr—gofyn iddi —— (*Rises.*)

KNOX. Why issn't there any geography now?
PUGH. Friday geography, Thursday today ——
CONIBEAR. Pnawn dydd Iau, te, hanner awr wedi tri ——

IDWAL. Dyma'r fistress! (MISS MOFFAT *walks in from garden.—All
rise but* BESSIE. *She is more alert and business-like than ever, is
studying exercise book. She goes into kitchen.*)
SARAH. Miss Moffat.
DILL. Oh, yes.

(*The following fourteen speches spoken together.*)

PUGH.   Mi ddylaswn fod yn pobi heddyw—
             A dwidi gadal y cig yn y popdy—

KNOX. Mi fydd eich cegin chi ar dan, Mrs. Pugh ——
IDWAL. 'Nhad, gai fynd i chwara yn nghae John Davies ——
MCINERNEY. (*Answering him. Exit* DILL.) Ddim heddyw—dwisho
ti gartre ——

ROMANO. Yforty d'wi am drio sgwennu llythyr —— (*Crossing
to* CARTER.)
CARTER. Os gynnachi steel-pen golew?
MORGAN. Mae'na gymaint o flots!
NORMAN. Dwi wedi sgwennu llythyr at fy nain, wni ddim be
ddidi'thi.
MORGAN. Welsochi 'rioed eiriau fel one?

PUGH. Fedri'thi ddim canu fel Cymraes, digon siwr ——
ROBBATCH. Mae'r hen ddyn am ofyn rwbeth iddi eto—drychwch
arno ——
PUGH. Mi gollith'o ei Gymraeg cyn bo hir —— Idwal, what you
looking so sorry—always wanting to know something ——

NORMAN. Mae genni just ddigon o amswer i gyrraedd at y llyn—
             Mae'r dwr yn rhy oer i ymdrochi—
PUGH. Nag ydi—mae'r haul wedi bod yn rhy boeth heddyw —— (*The* CROWD *finally trickle out, shepherded by* MISS
RON. *Besides* BESSIE, *there are left* OLD TOM, *studying* MISS RON.
and IDWAL. MISS RON. *finds herself with* OLD TOM *and* IDWAL.)

38

IDWAL. (*Comes down a step.*) Miss Ronberry, please, what is four times fourteen?

MISS RON. Thank you so much for the flowers, Idwal, dear. (*Crosses to down* C. L. *of* TOM.)

IDWAL. Yes, Miss Ronberry. (*He follows the others out, leaves door open.*)

MISS RON. Is there anything you would like to know? (*Back a step.*) Mr. Tom?

OLD TOM. Where iss Shakespeare?

MISS RON. Where? . . . Shakespeare, Mr. Tom, was a very great writer.

OLD TOM. Writer? (MISS RON. *turns front.*) Like the Beibl?

MISS RON. Like the Bible.

OLD TOM. Dear me— (*Rises.*)—and me thinkin' the man was a place. (*Crosses up* C.) If I iss been born fifty years later, I iss been top of the class. (*Exits,* MISS RON. *follows him up.*)

MISS RON. Oh, dear. . . . (*Crosses via back to above first desk, clears large table, then to* L. *of it.* BESSIE *crawls over seats to small desk, sits.*) Miss Moffat has been doing grammar with Form Two under the pear-tree for an hour, she must be dead. . . . (*Stops.*) Why did you not get up when she crossed?

BESSIE. My foot went to sleep. (*At small desk* R.)

MISS RON. That, dear, is a naughty fib. (*Crosses to* L. *end of* L. *table.*)

BESSIE. (*Sits.*) If you want to know, Miss Ronberry, I feel quite faint sometimes, as if my heart'd stopped and the world was coming to an end.

MISS RON. (*At* L. *of large table.*) Bessie dear, how *horrid!* (*Crosses up to alcove.*)

JONES. It may be in the nature of a premonition.

MISS RON. A what?

JONES. I had a premonition once. Like a wave of the ocean breakin' on a sea-shell. Something had said to me that mornin': (MISS MOFFAT *enters from kitchen.*) "Walk, and think, and keep off the food, for thirteen hours." So I ordered my supper, and I went. Towards the end of the day, I was sittin' on a stile in a cloak of meditation; and a voice roared at me: "John Goronwy Jones, tomorrow morning is the end of the world!"

MISS MOFFAT. And was it?

JONES. It was eight years ago. It was a splendid experience.

MISS MOFFAT. (*Crosses to* L. *of* L. *table.*) Which proves how

39

much the gift of prophecy can owe to an empty stomach. . . .
Anybody seen a Greek book? (*Picking up tiny volume.*) Here it
is. . . . (*Starting to stairs.*)

MISS RON. Greek, Miss Moffat?

MISS MOFFAT. Morgan Evans is starting Greek this month.

MISS RON. No! I didn't know you knew Greek?

MISS MOFFAT. I don't; I've just got to keep one day ahead of him
and trust to luck. (*She disappears into her bedroom.*)

MISS RON. (*Sits desk in alcove.*) To think that two years ago he
hardly knew English!

BESSIE. Stuck-up teacher's pet.

MISS RON. You must not think that, dear. Miss Moffat says he is
clever.

BESSIE. He always looks right through me, so I don't know, I'm
sure. Stuck-up teacher's pet. . . . I got some scent on my hands,
Mr. Jones; like to smell them?

JONES. No, thank you, Bessie, I can smell them from here, thank
you.

BESSIE. Ooh, it's lovely. . . .

MISS RON. She has some wonderful plans for him—I can tell by
her manner. I think she is trying to send him to one of those
Church schools so that he can get a curateship. Would not that
be exciting?

BESSIE. I think she's ridin' for a fall. (JONES *turns, looks and goes
back to his work.*)

MISS RON. Bessie! Why? (*Crosses in to above No. 1 desk.*)

BESSIE. All this orderin' 'im about. I've got eyes in my head, if
she hasn't, and he's gettin' sick of it. I think a lady ought to be
dainty. She's no idea. (MISS MOFFAT *appears at top of stairs.*)

MISS MOFFAT. Evans! (*Calls, then appears. A pause.* MORGAN
*comes in from study. Crosses to below stairs. He is now seven-
teen. He is dressed in a shabby country suit, and is at the moment the submissive schoolboy, very different from the first act.
He carries a sheet of writing and a pen.* MISS MOFFAT'S *attitude
to him seems purely impersonal.* OTHERS *watch them.*) Finished?

MORGAN. Yes, Miss Moffat. (MISS RON. *sits on alcove desk again.
Rubs ink off her hands with pumice stone.*)

MISS MOFFAT. How many pages?

MORGAN. Nine.

MISS MOFFAT. Three too many. Boil down to six. Have you got
those lines of Voltaire?

MORGAN: Yes, Miss Moffat.

MISS MOFFAT. It's just five—have your walk now, good and brisk. . . . (MORGAN *taking his cap from a peg upstage of door* L. 1, *starts to cross* R. *via front.*)

MORGAN. Yes, Miss Moffat. (*Stops.*)

MISS MOFFAT. But kill two birds and get the Voltaire by heart. If you can ever argue a point like that, you'll do. (MORGAN *starts again.*) Back in twenty minutes—and take your pen from behind your ear. (*He takes pen and throws it on desk. She disappears into her bedroom.*)

BESSIE. Now turn a somersault and beg. (*Pause.* MORGAN *crosses to above small desk.* BESSIE *looks away from them all. Suddenly soft and mysterious.*) Can you smell scent?

MORGAN. Yes.

BESSIE. Nice, isn't it?

MORGAN. I don't know, I never come across scent before. (*Faces front.*) I did never come across . . . scent before. . . .

BESSIE. Bright, aren't you? Don't you ever get tired of lessons? (JONES *looks in disapproval. She begins to sing song, " With his bell bottom trousers."* MORGAN *crosses to* R. *door. He goes to front door, turns, then goes, banging door.* BESSIE *bangs book on desk.*) There we go. And my Mummy ought to be back soon, and then we'll know somethin'.

JONES. What is the matter? Where has she gone?

BESSIE. One of her prayer meetings. Twenty miles to shake a tambourine in the open air. I think it's wicked. . . . She ought to be just in time, and then we'll know.

JONES. Know what?

BESSIE. About that horrid Morgan Evans. It's been lessons every night with teacher, hasn't it, since we left the mine? And long walks in between, to blow the cobwebs away? But the last week or two we've been breaking our journey, so we've heard.

JONES. How do you mean?

BESSIE. A glass of rum next door at the Gwesmor Arms and then another, and then another!

JONES. (*Perturbed.*) Oh . . . (*Rises—crosses to* L. *of her, turns.*) Whoever told you that?

BESSIE. A little bird. (JONES *crosses to* L. C. *front of couch.*) And if my Mummy's sciatica's better she's going to jump up and look over the frosty part, and then we'll know. (MRS. WATTY *hurries in through front door, in high spirits. She wears an ill-fitting Mili-*

41

tant *Rigbteousness Corps uniform, and carries an umbrella and a
brown paper parcel.*)

MRS. WATTY. (*Comes in* R. *of No. 2 desk.* JONES *crosses to corner
of No. 1 desk.*) Guess what's 'appened to me!

BESSIE. What?

MRS. WATTY. I'm a Sergeant-Major! (MISS MOFFAT *has come out
on to landing, ber bair is down and she is brushing it.*)

MISS MOFFAT. Watty, you're not! (JONES *turns to* MISS MOFFAT.)

MRS. WATTY. Oh, Ma'am, I didn't see you —— (*Crosses to
above* L. *of table* L.)

MISS MOFFAT. Tell me more! (MISS RON. *rises.*)

MRS. WATTY. You remember Sergeant-Major 'Opkins desertin' in
Cardiff and marryin' a sailor?

MISS MOFFAT. Yes?

MRS. WATTY. Well, (*Crosses* JONES C.) last week, not two months
after she give up the Corpse, she was dead!

MISS MOFFAT. And you've stepped into her shoes?

MRS. WATTY. They're a bit on the big side; but I can put a bit of
paper in. The uniform fits lovely, though. (JONES *crosses to* R.
desk.) I'll get you a cup o' tea and an egg, Ma'am, you never 'ad
that cold meat, Ma'am, I'll be bound? (*Opens door* L. 2.)

MISS MOFFAT. Folk eat too much anyway. (*She goes back into ber
bedroom.*)

BESSIE. Did you jump? (JONES *turns attention to* WATTY.)

MRS. WATTY. (*Coming back into room, crosses down* L. *of couch.*)
Just caught 'im. (*To* JONES, *sorrowfully.*) He was 'avin' a good
drink, sir. . . . (*Crosses front to* L. *of* BESSIE. JONES *crosses to
above table. To* BESSIE.) Don't you dare tell 'er, you little dollymop, or I'll rattle your bones —— (MISS MOFFAT *reappears and
comes downstairs.*)

MISS MOFFAT. (*Comes down foot of stairs.*) Was it a nice service,
Watty? (MISS RON. *comes down above No. 2 desk.*)

MRS. WATTY. Beautiful, Ma'am. They said they 'oped the late
Sergeant-Major was gone where we all want to go, but with 'er
having deserted they couldn't be sure. Then we saved three sin-
ners. You ought to been there . . . And the collection! (*Starts
for kitchen.*) I 'adn't seed so much oof since the Great Liverpool
Exhibition.

MISS RON. But they didn't make a collection at the Liverpool Exhibition, did they?

MRS. WATTY. No, but I did. (JONES *crosses via front to front of couch. Takes blackboard to settle.* MISS RON. *crosses down to small desk* U. C. MRS. WATTY *goes to kitchen.* MISS MOFFAT *crosses to* L. *of* BESSIE.)

BESSIE. Please, Miss Moffat, can I have the money for my ticket?

(JONES *draws diagram on blackboard.*)

MISS MOFFAT. What ticket?

BESSIE. For Tregarna Fair tomorrow. You said I could go.

MISS MOFFAT. On the contrary, I said you couldn't. (*To desk* R.) Not in school hours.

MISS RON. Are you feeling better, dear? (*Crosses* L. *above and* L. *of* BESSIE.)

BESSIE. No, Miss Ronberry. It's all this sittin' down. It's been going on for two years now. I heard tell it ends in everythin' rottin' away. (MISS MOFFAT *sits at desk.*)

MISS MOFFAT. What's rotting away?

MISS RON. (*Crosses toward* R. *a step.*) Bessie says she's been sitting down for two years.

MISS MOFFAT. She's lucky. My feet feel as if I've been standing for the same length of time. What are these, Ron? (MISS RON. *crosses to* L. *of* MISS MOFFAT.)

MISS RON. Two more accounts, I fear.

MISS MOFFAT. Oh, yes. The Liddell and Scott and Evans' new suit—tch. . . . (*Cheerfully.*) I shall have to sell out a couple more shares, I expect.

MISS RON. Oh, dear.

MISS MOFFAT. Not at all. It's easy to squander money, and it's easy to hoard it; the most difficult thing in the world is to use it. And if I've learned to use it, I've *done* something. That's better. . . . My plans are laid, Ron, my dear, my plans are laid! But don't ask me what I'm hatching, because I can't tell you till tomorrow.

MISS RON. You are wonderful!

MISS MOFFAT. Go to Halifax. (*Miss* RON. *crosses to and sits couch.*) I'm enjoying myself. (*Huge sigh from* BESSIE.) Bessie Watty, what is this dying duck business?

BESSIE. Yes, Miss Moffat.

MISS MOFFAT. Don't " yes, Miss Moffat," me. Explain yourself.

BESSIE. My Mummy said all these lessons is bad for my inside.

MISS MOFFAT. She told me they stop you eating sweets, but perhaps I am telling the lie.

BESSIE. Yes, Miss Moffat.

MISS MOFFAT. What's the matter with your inside?

BESSIE. It goes round and round through sittin' down. P'r'aps what I want is a change. (Back on her elbows.)

MISS MOFFAT. (Muttering.) "Adelphos, a brother" . . . There is nothing to prevent your going for walks between lessons. You can go for one now, as far as Sarah Pugh Postman, to see if my new chalks have arrived. (Pause.) Quick march. (BESSIE crosses up R. to door.)

BESSIE. I'm not goin'.

MISS MOFFAT. What did you say?

BESSIE. I'm not goin'. (Crosses down front of No. 1 desk.) Everybody's against me. . . . (Crosses in.) I'm goin' to throw myself off of a cliff, an' kill myself. . . . It'll make a nice case in the papers, me in pieces at the bottom of a cliff! . . . I'm goin' mad, mad, and I'm goin' to kill myself, nothin' goin' to stop me—stone dead at the bottom of a cliff—ah—ah—ah —— (MRS. WATTY striding in from kitchen with a cupful of cold water which she throws into BESSIE's face.)

MRS. WATTY. (To MISS MOFFAT.) I made a mess o' your rug, Ma'am, but it's worth it. (Crosses L. to L. of couch.) She's got bad blood, this girl, mark my word.

MISS RON. She'll catch her death!

MRS. WATTY. (Starts up L.) Nothing like cold water, Ma'am. I learnt that with her father. 'E was foreign, you know. (She goes back into kitchen. MISS MOFFAT rises—crosses to BESSIE.)

MISS MOFFAT. And how do you feel after that?

BESSIE. I can't remember anything. I'm in a comma.

MISS MOFFAT. (Taking her by arm, starts L. with her to upstairs.) We'll sit on our bed for an hour with the door locked, shall we, and try to remember? And next week you go away into service— (JONES and MISS RON. look.)—and see how we like that —— (She pushes her out of sight into the passage, a door bangs, the noise of a lock turning. MISS MOFFAT comes downstairs, crossing to R. C., tucking key into her petticoat pocket.) I must count her as one of my failures. Fish out of water, of course. Guttersnipe species—if there is such a fish. (Stops C.) She'll be more at home in service. . . . (Muttering.) "Dendron, a tree ——"

MISS RON. I beg your pardon? . . . Oh, Miss Moffat, I am bursting with curiosity—your plans for Morgan Evans . . . is it a curateship?

MISS MOFFAT. (*Slowly, amused.*) No, it isn't a curateship. (*Crosses to desk* R.)

MISS RON. I really don't see anything funny about curates. (*To* JONES.) I mean, there is nothing *wrong* with curates, is there?

JONES. (*At settle below stairs.*) No, except that they ought to go to chapel.

MISS MOFFAT. Who has been writing in here? (MRS. WATTY appears at kitchen door.)

MRS. WATTY. Your egg, Ma'am!. (*Crosses to back of table* L.)

MISS MOFFAT. "Bessie Watty has the face of an angel!" (JONES takes hat from peg, crosses via back to R. U. door.)

MISS RON. What an extraordinary ——

MISS MOFFAT. But I know the writing —— (*Crosses up to him.*) John Goronwy Jones, I'm ashamed of you. (*Crosses him to up* C.)

JONES. I shall see you tomorrow if we are spared.

MISS RON. (*Shocked.*) Oh!

JONES. You all misjudge that little girl. She has the face of a good woman in the melting pot.

MISS MOFFAT. (*Crossing to kitchen.*) I've got the face of a good woman, too, and well out of the melting pot, but I don't think I'd ever find it in writing. (*She goes into kitchen.*)

MRS. WATTY. I never thought I'd live to call *you* a naughty man. (*She follows* MISS MOFFAT *into kitchen.* JONES *goes out through front door.* MISS RON. *crosses up* L., *gets her hat and shawl and crosses to small mirror in bookcase* R. *Front door opens abruptly and* MORGAN *appears. He is dishevelled, and it is fairly apparent that he has been drinking. His manner is defiant. The door bangs behind him.*)

MISS RON. Oh, it's you, Morgan. . . . (*Back at mirror.*) Miss Moffat is having something to eat.

MORGAN. And I have been having something to drink, so we are quits. (*Crosses down* R. C.)

MISS RON. I will tell her that you are back —— (*Crosses via front to* L. *of couch.*)

MORGAN. I don't want to see no Miss Moffat. (*Crosses down to desk chair.*)

MISS RON. You mean "I don't want to see Miss Moffat." The double negative —— (*Starts up* L. *back of couch.*)

MORGAN. Now don't you start! . . . (*Crosses* C. *via above small desk.*) I like the double negative, it says what I want the way I like, and I am *not* goin' to stand *no* interference from *nobody!*

45

Voltaire indeed . . . (*Crumples paper, kicks it, crosses* R. *all the way.*)

MISS RON. Morgan! I've never seen you like this before! (*Crosses up back of table* L. C.)

MORGAN. You haven't, have you? Well—(*Crosses up* R.)—now I come to think of it, I haven't neither, not for two years, and I'm surprised by meself, and shocked by meself! (*Crosses* L. *two steps.*) Goin' inside one o' them public houses and puttin' me nice clean boots on that dirty rail, and me dainty lady-fingers on that detestable mucky counter! Pourin' poison rum down me nice clean teeth—(*Down two steps.*)—and spittin' in a spittoon—what's come over you, Morgan Evans? (*Crosses down* R. C.) You come back to your little cage, and if you comb hair and wash hands and get your grammar right and forget you was once the Middle-weight Champion of the Glasynglo Miners, we might give you a nice bit of sewin' to do. . . . (*Down* R. *again.*) Where's (*Crosses* C.) that Bessie Watty, sendin' her mother to spy on me? I'll (*Goes front of couch.*) knock her bloody block off. . . .

MISS RON. (*Outraged.*) Morgan Evans, *language!* Don't you dare use an expression like that to me again!

MORGAN. (*Facing her, leaning over couch.*) I got plenty of others, thank you, and they are all comin' out. I am goin' to surprise quite a few —— (MISS MOFFAT *enters from kitchen.*)

MISS MOFFAT. Have a good walk, Evans? (*Crosses in to front of couch.*)

MORGAN. Yes, Miss Moffat.

MISS MOFFAT. Can you repeat the Voltaire? (*Sits couch.*)

MORGAN. Not yet.

MISS MOFFAT. It's very short.

MORGAN. Paper blowed away.

MISS MOFFAT. Oh. Copy it again, will you, and bring it to me.

MORGAN. (*Muttering.*) Yes, Miss Moffat. (*Crosses to door* L. 1.)

MISS MOFFAT. Would you like a drink? (MORGAN *stops.*)

MORGAN. No, thank you. (*He goes into study.*)

MISS MOFFAT. I hope he's not going to be slow at French. It'll make the Greek so much more difficult ——

MISS RON. (*Crosses in* R. *end table.*) You don't think perhaps all this—in his situation—is rather sudden for him? I mean ——

MISS MOFFAT. Not for him, my dear. He has the most brilliantly receptive brain I've ever come across. Don't tell him so, but he has.

MISS RON. I know *his* brain is all right ——

MISS MOFFAT. I'm very pleased with his progress, on the whole . . . (*A knock at front door.* MISS RON. *moves toward the door.* MISS MOFFAT *stops her.*) Wait a minute! (*Crosses up via L. to alcove window. Peering out toward front door.*) Yes, it is. . . .

MISS RON. Who?

MISS MOFFAT. Royalty, the Conservatives and all the Grand Lamas rolled into one. The Squire ——

MISS RON. The Squire! Oh, *my!*

MISS MOFFAT. It is·indeed, oh my —— Let me. have your shawl. (*Crosses over, gets shawl from* MISS RON., *crosses down to stairs.*)

MISS RON. (*To L. of large table.*) But he hasn't been here since that dreadful evening ——

MISS MOFFAT.. (*Going upstairs.*) I behaved more stupidly that night than I ever have in my life, and that's saying something ——

MISS RON. But why is he here now?

MISS MOFFAT. Never you mind. . . . All I can tell you is that it is to do with Morgan Evans, and that it is vital I make the right impression ——

MISS RON. (*As* MISS MOFFAT *runs upstairs.*) What sort of impression?

MISS MOFFAT. (*On last step.*) Helpless and clinging, or as near as dammit —— (*She disappears into her room, as there is a second impatient knock at front door.*)

MISS RON. Come in!

(*Door opens and* GROOM *appears.*)

GROOM. (*Announcing.*) The Squire. (*The* SQUIRE *follows the* GROOM *in.* GROOM *retires and shuts door.*)

SQUIRE. Good afternoon. (*He is dressed in a summer lounge suit, and holds his hat in his hand.*)

MISS RON. Your hat, Squire —— (*Crosses to* R. C., *front of No. 1 desk.*)

SQUIRE. No, thank you, I am not staying.

MISS RON. Oh, dear, I do look a sketch. . . . (*Moves back* L. C.)

SQUIRE. (*Looks around.*) So this is the seat of learning. (*Crosses down* R. C.)

MISS RON. (L. C.) We are always on the point of a good spring-clean. How dreadful that we have no refreshment to offer you!

SQUIRE. You can tell her from me that I am not here to be insulted again.

MISS RON. Oh, I'm sure you aren't! I mean ——

SQUIRE. (*Crosses to* R. *of small desk.*) She called me an addle-headed nincompoop. (MISS MOFFAT *comes downstairs, a lace shawl draped over her shoulder. She carries a bowl of flowers.*)

MISS MOFFAT. Miss Ronberry, dear, my roses are dying—would you pour out a little water for them, I have such a headache I don't think —— (*At foot of stairs, feigning surprise.*) Squire! (*Then crosses to* L. C., *front of couch.*)

SQUIRE. You wrote to me. Perhaps you have forgotten?

MISS MOFFAT. How could I forget! I only thought that after the overwrought fashion of my behavior at our last meeting you must ignore my very nervous invitation—Miss Ronberry, a chair, dear, for the Squire ——

(MISS RON. *takes small chair from small desk, places it* L. *of small desk.*)

SQUIRE. (*Crosses in to* L. *of chair.*) I have not a great deal of time to spare, I fear.

MISS MOFFAT. Of course you haven't. I was just saying to Miss Ronberry, he's so busy he'll *never* be able to fit it in! Miss Ronberry, dear, would you get some water for them? (*She hands bowl to* MISS RON., *who passes the* SQUIRE *and goes into garden.*) Tell me, Squire, how did your prize-giving fare this afternoon?

SQUIRE. Rather a bore, y'know.

MISS MOFFAT. I had so hoped to see you judge. I love flowers.

SQUIRE. It wasn't flowers. It was cows.

MISS MOFFAT. Oh. It was your speech I wanted to hear, of course; I heard you made such an amusing one at the Croquet.

SQUIRE. Oh, did they tell you about that? Rather a good pun, eh? (*Laughing.*) Ha, ha . . . I—may I sit down? (*He sits chair* L. *of small desk, getting rid of hat.*)

MISS MOFFAT. Do!

SQUIRE. I thought Griffith, the butcher, was going to laugh his napper off.

MISS MOFFAT. Indeed . . . Do you know, Squire, that makes me rather proud?

SQUIRE. Proud? Why?

MISS MOFFAT. Because he would not have understood a word if his little girls hadn't learnt English at my school.

SQUIRE. Oh. Never thought of it like that. . . . (*As she puts her hand to her head, says* "Oh.") Headache?

48

MISS MOFFAT. Squire, you see before you a tired woman. We live and learn, and I have learnt how right you were that night. I have worked my fingers to the bone battering my head against a stone wall.

SQUIRE. But I heard you were a spiffing success.

MISS MOFFAT. Oh, no.

SQUIRE. (*Muttering.*) It's fair of you to admit it, I must say.

MISS MOFFAT. You see, in one's womanly enthusiasm one forgets that the qualities vital to success in this sort of venture are completely lacking in one: intelligence, courage and authority . . . the qualities, in short, of a man.

SQUIRE. Come, come, you mustn't be too hard on yourself, y'know. After all, you've meant well.

MISS MOFFAT. It's kind of you to say that.

SQUIRE. What about this Jones chappie?

MISS MOFFAT. He's a dear creature, but . . . I have no wish to be fulsome, I mean a man like yourself.

SQUIRE. I see.

MISS MOFFAT. One gets into such muddles! You'd never believe!

SQUIRE. Well . . . I've never been on your side, but I'm sorry to hear you've come a cropper. When are you giving it up?

MISS MOFFAT. Oh . . . That again is difficult; I have all my widow's mite, as it were, in the venture —— (MORGAN *appears from study carrying a paper. He has regained his self-control.*)

MORGAN. (*Stops.*) Please excuse me ——

MISS MOFFAT. It's all right, Evans. Have you copied it? On my desk, will you? (EVANS *crosses front to desk* R.)

MORGAN. Excuse me, sir. . . . (*Stops.*) Good afternoon, sir.

SQUIRE. Good afternoon, my boy.

MORGAN. Excuse me, sir. . . . (*Crosses back to study* L. 1, *stops at* L. *of couch. Turning at study door.*) Thank you. (*He goes.*)

SQUIRE. Nice, well-spoken lad. Relative?

MISS MOFFAT. No. A pupil. He used to be one of your miners.

SQUIRE. No! Is that so?

MISS MOFFAT. I'm glad you thought he was a nice, well-spoken lad.

SQUIRE. Yes . . . One of my miners, interesting . . .

MISS MOFFAT. Because he is the problem I should like your advice about.

SQUIRE. What's he been up to, poaching?

MISS MOFFAT. No.

SQUIRE. A bit o' muslin?

MISS MOFFAT. No, no . . . There are none, anyway ——

SQUIRE. What about the little Cockney filly?

MISS MOFFAT. Bessie Watty? Oh, no, I assure you—she's a school girl ——

SQUIRE. I dunno, all these young people growing up together, y'know—eh?

MISS MOFFAT. I think it's good for them. . . . No, there's nothing of that sort—but he's a problem just the same. And like a true woman I have to scream for help to a man. To you.

SQUIRE. (*Gives away here.*) Scream away, dear lady, scream away!

MISS MOFFAT. Well, he's . . . clever.

SQUIRE. Oh, is he? Good at figures, and all that? Because if he is, there's no reason why I shouldn't put him in my mine office, as junior office boy. What d'ye think of that?

MISS MOFFAT. No. Figures aren't his strong point.

SQUIRE. Thought you said he was clever.

MISS MOFFAT. To begin with, he can write.

SQUIRE. Oh. Well?

MISS MOFFAT. Very well.

SQUIRE. Then he could make fair copies. Eh?

MISS MOFFAT. No. (*Choosing her words carefully.*) This boy . . . is quite out of the ordinary.

SQUIRE. Sure?

MISS MOFFAT. As sure as one of your miners would be, cutting through coal and striking a diamond without a flaw. He was born with very exceptional gifts. They must be—they ought to be given every chance.

SQUIRE. You mean he might turn into a literary bloke?

MISS MOFFAT. He might, yes.

SQUIRE. I'm blowed! How d'ye know?

MISS MOFFAT. By his work. It's very good.

SQUIRE. How d'ye know it's good?

MISS MOFFAT. How does one know Shakespeare's good?

SQUIRE. Shakespeare? What's he got to do with it?

MISS MOFFAT. He was a literary bloke.

SQUIRE. Ye-es. *He* was good, of course.

MISS MOFFAT. This tenant of yours, Squire, has it in him to bring great credit to you.

SQUIRE. Yes, he *is* a tenant of mine, isn't he?

MISS MOFFAT. Imagine if you could say that you had known—well, say Lord Tennyson, as a boy on your estate!

SQUIRE. Rather a lark, what? Though it's a bit different, y'know, Tennyson was at Cambridge. My old college.

MISS MOFFAT. Oh . . . (*Rises, crosses R. via front to bookcase R.* SQUIRE *rises.*) Poor Evans. What a pity he was not born at the beginning of the eighteenth century!

SQUIRE. Beginning of the eighteenth century—now when was that . . . ? (*Crosses front of couch.*)

MISS MOFFAT. He would have had a protector. (*Takes two books from bookcase.*)

SQUIRE. What against?

MISS MOFFAT. A patron. (*Crosses to R. of him.*) Pope, you recall, dedicated the famous " Essay on Man " to his protector. (*Crosses front of small desk, hands him books.*)

SQUIRE. (*Reading from book.*) "To H. St. John Lord Bolingbroke." Mmm . . . I *have* heard of it, now I remember ——

MISS MOFFAT. Isn't it wonderful to think that that inscription is handed down to posterity? (*Reading from other book.*) " To the Right Honorable Earl of Southampton . . . Your Honor's in all duty, William Shakespeare."

SQUIRE. Oh!

MISS MOFFAT. I often think of the pride that surged in the Earl's bosom when his encouragement gave birth to the masterpiece (*Crosses to L. of couch.*) of a poor and humble writer!

SQUIRE. Funny, (*Crosses, sits couch.*) I never thought of Shakespeare being poor, somehow.

MISS MOFFAT. Some say his father was a butcher. The Earl realized he had genius, and fostered it.

SQUIRE. Mmm! If this boy really is clever, it seems a pity for *me* not to do something about it, doesn't it?

MISS MOFFAT. A great pity. (*Crossing, sits L. of* SQUIRE *on couch.*) And I can tell you exactly how you *can* do something about it.

SQUIRE. How?

MISS MOFFAT. There's a scholarship going.

SQUIRE. Scholarship? Where?

MISS MOFFAT. To Oxford.

SQUIRE. Oxford?

MISS MOFFAT. (*Moves closer.*) A scholarship to Trinity College, Oxford, open to boys of secondary education in the British Isles.

My school hardly comes under the heading of secondary education, and I wrote to your brother at Magdalen; he pulled some strings for me, and they have agreed to make a special case of this boy, on one condition. That you vouch for him. Will you?

SQUIRE. My dear lady, you take the cake. . . . Can't he be just as clever at home?

MISS MOFFAT. No, he can't. For the sort of future he ought to have, he must have polish—he has everything else. The background of a university would be invaluable to him. . . . (SQUIRE *rises.*) Will you?

SQUIRE. (*Crosses to* L. *of small desk.*) Well, the "Varsity," (*Crosses* R.) y'know, hang it all . . . mind you, he'll never get it.

MISS MOFFAT. I know, but he *must* have the chance ——

SQUIRE. (*Crosses to between table and chair to foot of No. 2 desk.*) Still, y'know, even the mere prospect of one o' my miners ——

MISS MOFFAT. Think of Shakespeare!

SQUIRE. All serene. (MISS MOFFAT *rises.*) I'll drop a line to Henry next week. Rather a (*Crosses in for hat from No. 1 desk.*) lark, what? I must be off —— (*Crosses halfway up to door.*)

MISS MOFFAT. (*Crosses* C. *to below No. 1 desk.*) I should be most obliged if the letter could be posted tomorrow. Would you like me to draft out a recommendation and send it over to the Hall? You must be so busy with the estate ——

SQUIRE. I am rather. Polka supper tomorrow night. . . . Yes, do do that. (*Starts up to door.*) Good-bye, dear lady!

MISS MOFFAT. (*Crosses in a step.*) Thank you so very much, Squire ——

SQUIRE. (*Crosses halfway down.*) Happier conditions, and all that! Glad you've come to your senses! (*Crosses up to door.*)

MISS MOFFAT. Thank you so very much, Squire!

SQUIRE. Not at all, I'm all for giving a writer-fellow a helping hand. Tell my brother that, if you like. . . . (*Exits. Leaves door open.* MISS MOFFAT *crosses up, closes door.* MISS RON. *hurries in from garden, carrying bowl of roses.*)

MISS RON. Well? (*Puts vase on desk.*)

MISS MOFFAT. (*Up* R. *below door.*) That man is so stupid it sits on him like a halo.

MISS RON. What happened? (*Crosses to* R. *of* MISS MOFFAT.)

MISS MOFFAT. In ten minutes I have given the Squire the impres-

sion that he spends his whole time fostering genius in the il-
literate. (*Crosses* C.)

MISS RON. But how?

MISS MOFFAT. Soft soap and curtseying; with my brain, my heart
and my soul. (*Crosses up* C.) I've beaten you at your own game,
my dear; (*Crosses* R. *between large and small desks.*) I flirted
with him! And he is going to write to Oxford; at least, (*Crosses
to chair back of table* L.) I am going to write to Oxford for him.
Hallelujah.

MISS RON. Oxford?

MISS MOFFAT. I am entering my little pit-pony for a scholarship
to Oxford, child, Oxford University!

MISS RON. But they don't have miners at Oxford University!

MISS MOFFAT. Well, they're going to. The lad is on this earth for
eighty years at the most, out of a few millions; (*Crosses down* L.)
let the proud silly ones grovel and be useful for a change, so he
can step up on their backs to something better! I was bursting to
say that to the Lord of the Manor—so I must vent it on you. . . .
Thank you for your shawl, my dear—(*Crosses to her. Takes her
to door up* R.)—and now you've served your purpose, you can go
home—but you'd better watch out, I may beat you to the altar
yet —— (*She shuts front door on her, and comes back into room,
crosses to desk* R., *gets papers, then crosses to* L. *table—moves
table, moves milk jug to sideboard upstage, sits back of table.
Seated before she calls.*) Evans! (MORGAN *comes in from study,
carrying a pen, books and papers.* MORGAN *crosses, gets small
chair at* R. C., *places it* L. *of* L. *table, sits. The daylight begins to
wane.*) Is this your essay on the Wealth of Nations?

MORGAN. Yes.

MISS MOFFAT. Say so and underline it. Nothing irritates examiners
more than that sort of vagueness. (*Pauses. She hands him exercise
book.*) I couldn't work this sentence out. (*Hands him paper.*)

MORGAN. " The eighteenth century was a cauldron. Vice and ele-
gance boiled to a simmer until the kitchen of society reeked ful-
minously, and the smell percolated to the marble halls above."
(*Hands paper back.*)

MISS MOFFAT. D'ye know what that means?

MORGAN. Yes, Miss Moffat.

MISS MOFFAT. Because I don't. Clarify, my boy, clarify, and
leave the rest to Mrs. Henry Wood. . . . " Water " with two
t's . . . that's a bad lapse. . . . The Adam Smith sentence was

good. Original, and clear as well. Seven out of ten, not bad but not good—you *must* avoid long words until you know exactly what they mean. Otherwise domino. . . . Your reading?

MORGAN. Yes, Miss Moffat.

MORGAN. Burke's " Cause of the Present Discontents."

MISS MOFFAT. Style?

MORGAN. His style appears to me . . . as if there was too much of it.

MISS MOFFAT. His style struck me as florid.

MORGAN. His style struck me as florid.

MISS MOFFAT. Again.

MORGAN. His style struck me as florid.

MISS MOFFAT. Subject matter?

MORGAN. A sound argument, falsified by—by the high color of the sentiments.

MISS MOFFAT. Mmmm. " The high color of the sentiments " . . . odd but not too odd, good and stylish. . . . For next time. (*Dictating.*) Walpole and Sheridan as representatives of their age; and no smelly cauldrons. (*Opening another book.*) By the way, next Tuesday I'm starting you on Greek.

MORGAN. Oh, yes?

MISS MOFFAT. I am going to put you in for a scholarship to Oxford.

MORGAN. Oxford? Where the lords go?

MISS MOFFAT. The same. (*Rises, crosses to desk* R., *looks above them below desk.*) I've made a simplified alphabet to begin with. It's jolly interesting after Latin. . . . Have a look at it by Tuesday, so we can make a good start—oh, and before we go on with the lesson, I've found the nail-file I mentioned—(MORGAN *slams a book.*)—I'll show you how to use it. I had them both here somewhere——

MORGAN. I shall not need a nail file in the coal mine.

MISS MOFFAT. In the what?

MORGAN. (*Turns to her.*) I am going back to the coal mine.

MISS MOFFAT. I don't understand you. Explain yourself.

MORGAN. I do not want to learn Greek, nor to pronounce any long English words, nor to keep my hands clean.

MISS MOFFAT. (*Crosses* C. *to lower end of* No. 1 *desk.*) What's the matter with you? Why not?

MORGAN. Because . . . because (*Leans over, both hands on table.*)—I was born in a Welsh hayfield when my mother was

54

helpin' with the harvest—and I always lived in a little house with no stairs, only a ladder—and no water—and until my brothers was killed I never sleep except three in a bed. I know that is terrible grammar but it is true.

MISS MOFFAT. What on earth has three in a bed got to do with learning Greek?

MORGAN. It has—a lot! The last two years I have not had no proper talk with English chaps in the mine because I was so busy keepin' this old grammar in its place. Tryin' to better myself . . . tryin' to better myself, the day and the night! . . . You cannot take a nail file into the " Gwesmor Arms " public bar!

MISS MOFFAT. My dear boy, file your nails at home! I never heard anything so ridiculous. Besides, you don't go to the Gwesmor Arms!

MORGAN. Yes, I do, I have been there every afternoon for a week, spendin' your pocket money, and I have been there now, (*Rises.*) and that is why I can speak my mind! (*Two steps* L.)

MISS MOFFAT. I had no idea that you felt like this.

MORGAN. Because you are not interested in me.

MISS MOFFAT. Not interested in you?

MORGAN. How can you be interested in a machine that you put a penny in and if nothing comes out you give it a good shake? " Evans, write me an essay; Evans, get up and bow; Evans, what is a subjunctive? " My name is Morgan Evans, and all my friends call me Morgan, and if there is anything gets on the wrong side of me it is callin' me Evans! . . . And do you know what they call me in the Village? (*Crosses front couch* L.) Ci bach yr ysgol! The schoolmistress's little dog! What has (*Crosses to her.*) it got to do with you if my nails are dirty? Mind your own business! (*Sits sofa, head in hand, faces* L. MISS MOFFAT *turns up to No. 2 desk.*)

MISS MOFFAT. I never meant you to know this. I have spent money on you—I don't mind that, (MORGAN *moves.*) money ought to be spent. But time is different. Your life has not yet begun, mine is half over. And when you're a spinster, some folk say it's pretty near finished. Two years is valuable currency. I have spent two years on you. (MORGAN *changes position of head, looks around.*) Ever since that first day, the mainspring of this school has been your career. Sometimes, in the middle of the night, when I have been desperately tired, I have lain awake, making plans. Large and small. Sensible and silly. Plans for you. And you tell

55

me I have no interest in you. If I say any more I shall start to cry; and I haven't cried since I was younger than you are, and I'd never forgive you for that. (*Crosses up to door—gets cloak.*) I am going for a walk. I don't like this sort of conversation, please never mention it again. If you want to go on, be at school tomorrow. (*Going.*) If not, don't.

MORGAN. I don't want your money, and I don't want your time! . . . I don't want to be thankful to no strange woman—for anything!

MISS MOFFAT. I don't understand you. I don't understand you at all. (*Putting on her cloak that is hanging on door. She goes out by front door.* MORGAN *folds his arms, takes a drink, puts bottle on table. There is a book there. He moves book.* BESSIE *comes in from garden. She has put her hair half up and wears earrings. She crosses in to* R. C., *front of No. 1 bench.*)

BESSIE. Hello! (*She clutches her leg.*) Caught my knee climbin' down the rainpipe, ooh . . . (*As he takes no notice. She crosses to kitchen door.*) P'r'aps I'm invisible. . . . (*She marches into kitchen, singing "*BELL BOTTOM TROUSERS*" and bangs door behind her. Far away, the sound of singing: men returning from the mine, harmonizing their familiar melody, "*YR HUFEN MELYN.*"* BESSIE *returns from kitchen, crosses to above No. 1 desk, leans on upper one.*) Mum's gone out. (*After a pause.*) Expect she's gone to tell Mrs. Roberts about her meetin'. Though how she manages with Mrs. Roberts knowin' no English an' deaf as well . . . (*After a pause.*) Talking a lot, aren't I?

MORGAN. Yes.

BESSIE. Well, I'm not deaf. (*Sits on table* R. *upper side.*)

MORGAN. Been spyin'?

BESSIE. If people lock me in and take the key out of the keyhole, they can't blame me for listenin' at it. (*Crosses down between table and desks to* R. C.) Oo, I think she's wicked.

MORGAN. Mind your own business!

BESSIE. I won't. I like to know about everything; I like doin' all the things I like, I like sweets, I don't care if it does make me fat, and I *love* earrings. (*Crosses to* L. *of small desk* R.) I like to shake my head like a lady. . . . (*Crosses* C. *Singing stops. A pause.*) It's funny. . . . (*Crosses* L. *front of him to* L.) We never been by ourselves before. (*Crosses up to alcove. She begins to sing in Welsh. The tune is "*Lliw Gwyn Rhosyn yr Haf.*" Crosses down* R. *of table in back—then down to* L. *of table, leans on*

56

chair. Sits on edge of table.) Didn't know I knew Welsh, did you?
. . . You like that song, don't you? That's why I learnt it.

MORGAN. You are different when you sing.

BESSIE. Am I? . . . What's this, medicine? (*Picks up rum bottle,
drinks. He takes bottle from her, takes a drink and puts it in his
pocket.*) Tastes like rubber. Nice, though. . . . (MORGAN *rises,
crosses* C.) You know—(*Crosses* C., L. *of him.*)—you was quite
right to put her in her place. Clever chap like you learnin' lessons off a woman!

MORGAN. (*Moves a step first.*) That's right. . . . (*Moves* R. *to
desk No. 2.*)

BESSIE. (*Crosses to* L. *of him.*) You don't 'ave to go to Oxford!
Clever chap like you!

MORGAN. That's right. . . . (*Crosses to desk* R.)

BESSIE. (*Crosses to him.*) What a man wants is a bit o' sym-
pathy! (*She sings again, backs away up stage and* L. *He follows
slowly and embraces her.*)

(CURTAIN FALLS, *and rises immediately* . . .)

ACT II

SCENE 2: *The same. A morning in November, three
months later. The room is much as it was, the potted
plants have been removed, the daylight is so poor that
the lamps are lit. The two small desks are cleared. Snow
cloth at up* R. *of door, large table moved* L., *lamp placed
on large table again, snow at windows, small desk chair
placed in* R. *upper corner.* R. C. *armchair moved to* L. 1
study door.

MRS. WATTY *is carrying in from kitchen a small table,
new and light. On it blotter, ink, pens, pencil, a duster
and a cup of tea.* MISS RONBERRY *is pushing armchair in
from study past sofa into its old place, next to the isolated desk.*

MRS. WATTY. (*Singing.*) I'm saved I am, I'm saved I am. . . .
(MRS. WATTY *moves large table* R. *a bit, so as to get through, picks
up small table, places it down* C.) What would the armchair be
for, Miss?

57

MISS RON. (*Places armchair at* R. C.) The Squire's coming. He's in-vigilating. (*Pushes desk chair into desk—opens desk drawer, takes out package with sealed Oxford papers.*)

MRS. WATTY. *What* was that, please, Miss?

MISS RON. The Oxford people have appointed him and Miss Moffat to watch Morgan Evans while he is sitting the scholarship, so that he cannot cheat.

MRS. WATTY. What a shame. . . . (*Looks out window. Crosses up, gets small chair from above desk, places it front of small table* C.) You'd never think it was nearly nine in the morning, would you? (*Crosses up* L. *to above table* L. C.)

MISS RON. It's stopped snowing.

MRS. WATTY. (*Looks out window.*) Only just. The milkman said the road was blocked down by the bridge. (*Straightens table, moves chair back of table to under table. Moves lamp to* R. *lower corner.*)

MISS RON. How terrible if Morgan couldn't get through!

MRS. WATTY. Countin' sheep all night, I was. (*Crosses to* R. U. *door. Picks up letter.*) She didn't 'ave a wink neither. I could 'ear her thinkin'.

MISS RON. It is a very important day for her.

MRS. WATTY. (*Crosses down* R.) Looks like that one's Bessie. Would you mind?

MISS RON. (*Crosses to her.*) That means Sarah the Post got through —— (*Crosses to desk for lamp light.*)

MRS. WATTY. She'd come the other way, down the 'ill ——

MISS RON. That's true . . . "Dear Mum"—to think I taught her to write—"Cheltenham is terrible. Can I have a shilling. I do the steps. Madam is terrible. Your obedient girl." (*Crosses to desk.*)

MRS. WATTY. Obedient. (*Laughs.*) I like that. . . . (*Crosses to waste-basket with letter.*) She's been away three months now, she ought to be gettin' used to it. (*Crosses to small table* C., *dusts* R. *side.*)

MISS RON. But do you not miss her?

MRS. WATTY. (*Looks at* MISS RON.) No! I don't like 'er, you know, never 'ave.

MISS RON. But, Mrs. Watty, your own daughter! (MRS. WATTY *crosses to* L. *of table, looks for dust, rubs spot off table.*)

MRS. WATTY. I know, but I've never been able to take to 'er. First time I saw 'er, I said—(*Shakes head.*)—"No." (*Crosses up* L. *to kitchen door. Going.*) With 'er dad being foreign, you see.

MISS RON. But couldn't your husband have taken her abroad to his own family?

MRS. WATTY. Oh, my 'usband was quite different. British to the core. (MISS RON. *turns.* MRS. WATTY *goes into kitchen.* MISS RON. *crosses to* R. *of small table* C., *then sits couch.* MISS MOFFAT *comes slowly downstairs.*)

MISS MOFFAT. (*Speaks as she crosses to desk.*) It's stopped snowing. (*Above desk.*)

MISS RON. It's a white world, as they say. . . . Do you think he will get through the snow?

MISS MOFFAT. This morning he would get through anything.

MISS RON. I am so glad. I thought perhaps he—he had not been working satisfactorily ——

MISS MOFFAT. At ten o'clock last night I had to take his books away from him.

MISS RON. I *am* glad.

MISS MOFFAT. I hope he won't get wet—he must not (*Picks up string, plays with it.*) be upset in any way. What made you think he wasn't working well?

MISS RON. Nothing, only . . . you remember the night you went for that long walk, when he might be going back to the mine?

MISS MOFFAT. (*After a pause.*) Yes?

MISS RON. The next morning he started studying again, and yet it seemed so different.

MISS MOFFAT. How?

MISS RON. Almost strained . . . what a silly thing to say . . . I mean, as you did not say anything more about the mine ——

MISS MOFFAT. He didn't say any more himself. He just turned up. I didn't embrace him on both cheeks, but I said "righto." Since which time he has never stopped working.

MISS RON. I *am* so glad. . . . Oh, this arrived from (MISS MOFFAT *crosses to her at couch.*) the Penlan Town Hall! It must be his birth certificate ——

MISS MOFFAT. Good. . . . (*Crosses back to desk via above* R. C. *armchair.*) I must send it off to the President of Trinity. Rather a nervous post mortem from him last night; two pages to ask if the youngster's legitimate; (*Opens envelope, looks at certificate.*) thank Heaven he is. And no conviction for drunkenness; references have been spotless. That will help, I hope.

MISS RON. Would it not be splendid if he . . . won!

MISS MOFFAT. (*After a pause.*) Not very likely, I am afraid.

(*Crosses up* R.) The syllabus rather attaches importance to general knowledge of the academic sort. His is bound to be patchy—on the exuberant side—I have had to force it; two years (*Crosses down* R.) is not enough even for him. (*Crosses to* C.) If he checks himself, and does not start telling them what they ought to think of Milton, with fair luck he might stand a chance. (*Crosses down* R.) He will have some pretty strong public school candidates against him, of course. Bound to. (*A step downstage.*) It depends on how much the examiners will appreciate a highly original intelligence.

MISS RON. (*Seated on couch.*) But wouldn't it be *exciting!*

MISS MOFFAT. (R. *at desk.*) Yes, it would. People run down the Universities, and always will, but it would be a wonderful thing for him. It would be a wonderful thing for rural education all over the country.

MISS RON. And most of all, it would be a wonderful thing for you!

MISS MOFFAT. (*Crosses to* L. *of armchair* R. C.) I suppose so. . . . It is odd to have spent so many hours with another human being, in the closest intellectual communion—because it has been that. I know every trick and twist of that brain of his, exactly where it will falter and where it will gallop ahead of me—and yet not to know him at all. I woke (*Crosses* R.) up in the middle of the night thinking of Henry the Eighth. I have a feeling there may be a question about the old boy and the Papacy. (*Crosses to bookshelves below desk. Takes book from shelf and makes notations on piece of writing paper.*) I'll cram one or two facts into him, the last minute. . . . Oh, God, he must win it. . . . (MRS. WATTY *comes in from kitchen, crosses to* L. *of* MISS MOFFAT.) He must . . .

MRS. WATTY. (*Hands her cup of tea.*) Cup a tea! Now, Ma'am, don't get in a pucker! (*Crosses* L. *via back.*) Six more Saturday mornin's like this in the next 'alf-year, (*Gets* MISS RON.'S *cup from table.*) remember!

MISS MOFFAT. The first paper is the important one—I expect we'll get more used to the others ——

MISS RON. Suppose the Squire doesn't come!

MISS MOFFAT. He will. He has got to the point of looking on the lad as a racehorse.

MISS RON. You don't think the snow might deter him?

MRS. WATTY. I (*Crosses to kitchen door.*) just seed 'is nibs' gardener clearin' a way from the gates. Shame the red carpet gettin' so wet. (MRS. WATTY *goes back into kitchen.*)

MISS RON. (*Crosses to desk.*) Surely it is getting brighter this side. . . . (*Looks out window.*) Oh, I can see him! Morgan, I mean!

MISS MOFFAT. Can you?

MISS RON. Coming up the Nant, do you see? Ploughing through!

MISS MOFFAT. What is the time? (*Looks at her breast watch.*)

MISS RON. Ten minutes to!

MISS MOFFAT. He will have just two minutes —— (*Sits at desk. A knock at front door.*) Good. There's the Squire ——

MISS RON. He is as excited as any of us —— (*Crosses up to open door, stands L. of door. BESSIE enters, followed by JONES.*) Bessie! . . . But it cannot be you, your mother has just received —— (*Backs away L. to C.*)

BESSIE. (*Crosses in to R. of small desks.*) I left the same day I posted it. (*She is shabbily dressed, in semi-grown-up fashion, and wears a cloak. Her manner is staccato, nervy and defiant. JONES closes door, leaves BESSIE's bag up R. above desk, then crosses in to L. of door.*)

MISS MOFFAT. This is unexpected.

BESSIE. Isn't it just? I have been travellin' all night, quite a wreck. I woke Mr. Jones up and he got the station-master to drive us over in his trap, in the snow; nice, wasn't it?

MISS MOFFAT. You have arrived at an inconvenient time. (*MISS RON. crosses L. above table.*)

BESSIE. Fancy. (*Crosses down to armchair R. C., sits.*)

MISS MOFFAT. Have you come to see your mother?

BESSIE. No. (*JONES crosses L. above No. 1 school desk.*)

MISS MOFFAT. Then why are you here?

BESSIE. Questions and answers, just like school again!

MISS MOFFAT. (*Crosses up a step.*) Why have you brought this girl here this morning?

JONES. I did not bring her, Miss Moffat, she brought me ——

MISS MOFFAT. (*Crosses to L. of R. C. armchair.*) Whom have you come to see?

BESSIE. You.

MISS MOFFAT. Me? (*Crosses R. a step. BESSIE does not speak.*) I can give you exactly one minute of my time. (*Crosses to R. desk. Pause.*) Is it money? (*As BESSIE does not answer. To JONES and MISS RON.*) Will you wait in the study? (*Crosses to R. of arm-*

chair. JONES *follows* MISS RON. *into study.*) One minute . . .
Quickly!

BESSIE. Why?

MISS MOFFAT. Morgan Evans is sitting for his Oxford examination
here this morning.

BESSIE. Well, 'e needn't.

MISS MOFFAT. What do you mean?

BESSIE. Because he won't ever be goin' to Oxford.

MISS MOFFAT. Why not?

BESSIE. Because there's goin' to be a little stranger. (*A pause.*)
I'm going to have a little stranger. (*Sniffles.*)

MISS MOFFAT. You're lying.

BESSIE. Doctor Brett, The Firs, Cheltenham. . . . (MISS MOFFAT
crosses L. *Looks* L.) And if you don't believe it's Morgan Evans,
you ask 'im about that night you locked me up—the night you had
the words with him!

MISS MOFFAT. I see. . . . (*A step* R. *at small table* C.) Why
couldn't I have seen before! (*Turns to her.*) Does he know?

BESSIE. I've come to tell 'im! I was ever so upset, of course, and
now I've lost me place—ooh, she was artful—he'll have to marry
me, or I'll show him up, 'cause I must give the little stranger a
name ——

MISS MOFFAT. (*Over to her.*) Stop saying " little stranger." If you
must have a baby, then call it a baby! . . . Have you told anybody?

BESSIE. Mr. Jones, that's all ——

MISS RON. (*Enters* L. 1.) The Squire is coming up the road! (*She
goes back into study.*)

BESSIE. I'll wait here for him.

MISS MOFFAT. For the next three hours he must not be disturbed.
You are not going to see him ——

BESSIE. You can't bully me, the way I am! (*Rises to* R. *of her.*)
'Asn't sunk in yet, 'as it? I'm teaching you something, am I? You
didn't know things like that went on, did you? Why? You couldn't
see what was goin' on under your nose, 'cause you're too busy
managin' everythin'! Well, you can't manage him any longer,
'cause he's got to manage me now, the way I am, he's got to ——

(JONES *pokes his head round study door, he is in a state of panic.*
MISS RON. *hovers behind him.*)

JONES. Morgan Evans has turned the corner up the hill ——

MISS RON. So there isn't much time! (JONES *follows* MISS RON. *back into study.*)

MISS MOFFAT. I'm afraid I am going to do a little managing now. You are going into the kitchen, where your mother will make you breakfast; you will then lie down, and as soon as this session is finished we will go upstairs and talk it all over when we are a little calmer. (*A knock at front door.*)

BESSIE. He's here! I got to see him! (BESSIE *starts up.* MISS MOFFAT *detains her.*)

MISS MOFFAT. If you try and disobey me, I shall not answer for the consequences. (*Holds her wrist.*)

BESSIE. You wouldn't dare lay a finger on me ——

MISS MOFFAT. Oh, yes, I would. If you attempt to stay in this room, or to blab to anybody about this before we have had that talk—even your mother—I am in a pretty nervous state myself this morning, and I shall strike you so hard that I shall probably kill you. . . . I mean every word of that. (*Crosses to kitchen door, opens door, steps into scene a few steps and waits for* BESSIE *to exit. Another knock.*)

BESSIE. (*Laughs.*) I don't mind. (*Crosses via front to kitchen.*) Three hours'll go soon enough. (*Laughs. She goes into kitchen.* MISS MOFFAT *shuts door after her, crosses to and opens front door. The* SQUIRE *enters, in Inverness cape and hat, stamping snow from his boots, he carries several periodicals, chiefly sporting and dramatic. The rest of scene is played very quickly.*)

MISS MOFFAT. (*Takes his coat and hat.*) So very sorry—how kind of you—such a dreadful day —— (*Hangs* SQUIRE's *coat on door.*)

SQUIRE. (*Crosses down to* R. *of small table* C.) Not at all, Mistress Pedagogue, anything for a lark. . . . Glad it isn't me, what? . . . (*Crosses to couch—sits.*) I've got a spiffy bit of news for you.

MISS MOFFAT. Yes?

SQUIRE. I've bought the barn from Sir Herbert, and we can move the whole shoot next door by March. What d'ye think?

MISS MOFFAT. Wonderful —— (*Crosses down to desk* R.)

SQUIRE. We can knock a door straight through here to the barn.— Aren't ye pleased about it?

MISS MOFFAT. (*As* MISS RON. *runs in from study.*) Yes, but you know, this examination, (*Knocks at front door.* MISS RON. *enters, crosses via back.*) rather worrying ——

MISS RON. Good morning, Squire! Terrible weather ——

SQUIRE. Beastly —— (MISS RON. *opens front door, then to* R. *of it, lets* MORGAN *in, closes door before she takes his overcoat, cap and muffler.*)

MISS MOFFAT. Wet?

MORGAN. No, thank you—good day, sir ——

MISS RON. Let me take your things —— (*She hangs his things on door then crosses via back to* L. *of couch.*)

MORGAN. Thank you —— (*Crosses down* R.)

MISS MOFFAT. Before I open the papers, I have a feeling they may bring up Henry the Eighth. Memorize these two facts, will you? (*Hands him paper.*)

MISS RON. (*Crosses to* L. *of small table* C., *puts down sprig of white heather.*) White heather—just a thought! (*She runs into study.*)

MORGAN. Thank you ——

SQUIRE. Good luck, my boy.

MORGAN. Thank you, sir ——

SQUIRE. Glad it isn't me! (MORGAN *hands her paper.*)

JONES. (*Pops his head round study door.*) Pob llwyddiant, ymachgeni!

MORGAN. Diolch —— (MISS MOFFAT *throws paper in basket.* JONES *goes back into study.* MORGAN *crosses to table* C., *sits.*)

MISS MOFFAT. Name and particulars, to save time. And don't get exuberant.

MORGAN. No.

MISS MOFFAT. Or illegible.

MORGAN. No. (*Pause.*)

SQUIRE. But aren't you going to wish my little protegé good fortune?

MISS MOFFAT. (*After pause, to* MORGAN.) Good luck.

MORGAN. Thank you. (*Clock begins to strike nine.*)

MISS MOFFAT. Ready? (*Takes shears, cuts envelope, crosses* R. *to* R. *of small table and places examination paper in front of him. Then crosses to armchair* R. C., *looking at duplicate paper of questions, smiles.*) Henry the Eighth! (*Sits* R. C. *armchair. She looks toward kitchen, then at* MORGAN.)

CURTAIN FALLS SLOWLY

ACT III

SCENE: *The same. An afternoon in July. Seven months later.*

The school has been moved next door, and the room is much less crowded, small table is back in window recess, armchair is in its old position, large table, however, is no longer behind sofa with its chair, its place being taken by three small school desks facing front door, between front door and bay window a blackboard on its easel faces audience at an angle, with " Elizabeth, known as Good Queen Bess" written on it in block letters.

AT RISE: JONES *stands in command beside blackboard. At two of school-desks sit* IDWAL *and* ROBBART, *each poring over his slate. On settle sit the* SQUIRE, *downstage, his arms folded like a pupil, his eyes fixed on* JONES, *and next to him* OLD TOM, *upstage, laboriously copying inscription on to his slate.* JONES *crosses to* IDWAL'S *desk then to* ROBBART'S *desk, looks at their work.*

OLD TOM. Elissabeth . . . known . . . as . . . what in goodness is a " k " doin' there, that iss a pussell for me —— (JONES *crosses back to blackboard.*)

JONES. "I wandered lonely as a cloud." From The Daffodils, by Wordsworth. (MISS RON. *hurries in from garden, crosses up to* L. *of* JONES.)

MISS RON. What is the capital of Sweden?

JONES. Stockholm.

MISS RON. Thank you. (*She hurries back into garden.*)

OLD TOM. Please, sir, how many L's in " daffodils " ?

SQUIRE. Damned if I know. (JOHN OWEN *comes in by study door.*)

JOHN. Please, Mistar Jones, Form Two Arithmetic Report—Miss Moffat says will you come in school with it. (*He goes back.* JONES *follows him through study after getting book and papers from sideboard.* SQUIRE *snores.*)

ROBBART. Mae o'n cysgu. Tyd. Idwal ——

OLD TOM. Plenty Welsh at home, not in the class please, by request, scoundrels and notty boys!

IDWAL. (*Rises.*) Squire iss 'avin' a snore. Nai ddangos rwbeth ichi —— (*He rises, runs to blackboard, takes chalk and duster, and swiftly rubs out and adds to inscription till it reads: "NO . . . GOOD . . . BESSIE."* SQUIRE *grunts. As he strikes period sticks his foot out.*)

JONES. (*Returns.*) Now history. (*Stumbles over* SQUIRE'S *foot. Crosses to blackboard.*) Excuse me . . . Elizabeth —— Who did this? (SQUIRE *crosses up to window.*)

IDWAL. Please, Mr. Jones, perhaps it iss some terrible dunce that want to know what iss Bessie Watty been doin' the last few months. (*A pause.*)

JONES. Whoever it was . . . (SQUIRE *starts* R.—*crosses* L. *of* JONES.) I am going to cane him! It was not you, sir, by any chance?

SQUIRE. Not guilty. . . . Bessie Watty? Little Cockney thing? Nice ankles?

JONES. I do not know, sir. . . . (*Boys snicker.*) Silence, boys! (JONES *crosses to boys.*) Where is my duster? (SQUIRE *crosses to desk* R., *looks out window.*)

SQUIRE. Still no sign of him.

JONES. You mean Morgan Evans, (*Boys look up.*) sir? He is not (SQUIRE *crosses front to settle* L., *sits.*) expected before the train leaving Oxford half-past one ——

SQUIRE. There's a sporting chance the Viva finished yesterday, and I sent the wagonette to meet the one-ten.

JONES. Do you think that he may know the result when he arrives?

SQUIRE. I doubt it, Miss Moffat said we'll hear by letter in a day or two. . . . Think (*Rises, crosses via front to door up* R., *gets hat from hook on door.*) I'll propel the old pins down the highway, just in case . . .

IDWAL. Please, sir, what sort of a place is Oxford?

SQUIRE. Dunno, I'm sure. Cambridge myself. (*Goes. Leaves door open.*)

JONES. (*At blackboard.*) Now history. Repeat after me ——

IDWAL. Please, Mr. Jones, tell us about Bessie Watty!

JONES. If you are kept in tomorrow, I will give you religion. Repeat after me —— (*School bell rings.*) Dismiss! (ROBBART *rises and straps books.* JONES *crosses to desk* R. SARAH *hurries in from front door. She is dressed in her best, in the traditional Welsh peasant costume with a steeple hat.)*

SARAH. Please, sir, have you got my father—(*Crosses to* OLD TOM *at settle* L.)—tiddona, 'nhad, ma'dy frwas di'n oeri ——

OLD TOM. English, daughter, in the class,, pliss!

SARAH. You are an old soft, your porridge it iss gettin' cold and you have not got your sleep ——

OLD TOM. But I got my Queen Elizabeth —— (SARAH *takes his slate, puts it on* ROBBART'S *desk.*)

SARAH. And in the mornin' you got your rheumatics—come on!

(SARAH *helps* OLD TOM *to rise.* MISS RON. *comes in from garden.*)

ROBBART. Sarah Pugh, (*Crosses to up* R. C.) what you all clobbered up for?

SARAH. Because for Morgan Evans.

(*Downstage of* TOM—*they cross otward* R.)

JONES. Is there some news? (*Crosses in to* R. *of armchair* R. C.)

MISS RON. About Morgan? Oh, quickly! (*Crosses to* R. *of* JONES.)

SARAH. (*Between couch and armchair.*) Not yet, Mistar Jones. But when it comes, I know it iss good news, so what do I do? I open the dresser, out the lavender bags and into my Sundays! Home, (*Starts up to door with* TOM.) dada, for Sundays ——

JONES. Before we have definite news, that is unwise ——

SARAH. John Goronwy Jones, pliss sir, you are an old soft. Everybody is ready to meet him by the Nant! The grocer got his fiddle ——

IDWAL. (*Rises.*) And William Williams the public got his cornet!

ROBBART. And with me on me mouth-organ —— (*Strikes chord on mouth-organ.*)

SARAH. And me singin'!

ROBBART. Tyd, Idwal —— (*He runs out by front door, followed by* IDWAL. JONES *crosses up and* L. *to small desk.*)

MISS RON. Perhaps preparing for news to be good means that it will be.

JONES. Everything is pre-ordained. Morgan Evans has either won the scholarship, or lost it.

MISS RON. Let us all say together, (JONES *moves out of scene.*) " Morgan Evans has won the scholarship! "

ALL. (*Except* JONES.) " Morgan Evans has won the scholarship! "

SARAH. Tiddana, 'nhad —— (*Crosses to* U. R. *of door.* OLD TOM *crosses to door.*)

OLD TOM. I never got a letter yet, and nobody never put Sundays on for me. . . . (*He goes out by front door.* SARAH *starts to go.* MISS RON. *crosses front to* R. *end of couch.*)

MISS RON. "No . . . (SARAH *comes back to* R. *of blackboard.* MISS RON. *crosses up to blackboard.*) good . . . Bessie." Good gracious!

JONES. Where is my duster? (*Looks behind blackboard.*)

MISS RON. What does that mean?

SARAH. (JONES *finds duster at* IDWAL'S *desk.*) Bessie Watty. Miss Ronberry, where is she?

MISS RON. I don't know, dear.

SARAH. Miss Moffat she hears from her, (JONES *erases blackboard.*) in my post office. (*Starts to go backing out.*) We wass all wonderin'. (*She goes out by front door.* JONES *crosses to desk* R.)

MISS RON. (*Crosses.*) Well, I have been wondering, too! (*Sits couch.*) She came back that morning and just went away again —— Morgan Evans was telling me only the day he left for Oxford that he didn't even *see* her. Where is she?

JONES. It is more important to know if Morgan Evans has won or not.

MISS RON. I know . . . if he hasn't, it will break her heart.

JONES. Would she feel it so keen as all that?

MISS RON. I used not to think so, (JONES *nods.*) but since that day they have been so much better friends, it has been a pleasure to hear them conversing—(JONES *turns back to work.*)—perhaps it is the strain of all these examinations —— (MISS MOFFAT *comes in from study with exercise book. Comes in to below settle* L.)

MISS MOFFAT. Gwyneth Thomas the plasterer's eldest; essay on Knowledge. "Be good, sweet maid, and let who will be clever ——" I wonder if the Reverend Kingsley had any idea what a smack in the eye that was for lady teachers? (*Crosses up* L. *of small desk.*) And then Gwyneth Thomas starts—(*Reading.*)—" It is not nice to know too much. I wish to be like Miss Ronberry, Miss Moffat is different, she knows everything." (*Crosses down to* MISS RON.) Any news?

JONES. Not yet.

MISS MOFFAT. I thought not. . . . (*A pause.*) Where is the Squire?

JONES. Gone to see if there is any sign.

MISS MOFFAT. (*Crosses* C.) Thank the Lord, that man is really becoming a nuisance. He gave up Henley to be here this week— (*Sits* R. *arm of couch.*)— did you know?

JONES. You do not appear nervous? (*Crosses to* R. *of armchair* R. C.)

MISS MOFFAT. I am past being nervous. If he has won, I shan't believe it. Flatly.

MISS RON. And if he has lost? (JONES *crosses back to* R. *desk.*)

MISS MOFFAT. If he has lost . . . (*After a pause.*) . . . we must proceed as if nothing had happened. The sun rises and sets every day, and while it does we have jolly well got to revolve round it; the time to sit up and take notice will be the day it decides not to appear. In the meantime, Mr. Jones, your report is on your desk; (JONES *crosses front to* L. 1 *with his bag and papers.*) Miss Ronberry, Form Two are waiting for your music like a jungle of hungry parakeets. (*Crosses up* R. C. MISS RON. *follows* JONES.)

MISS RON. Yes, Miss Moffat. (*They retire through study.* MISS MOFFAT *is alone. She crosses via back to* R. *of stairway. Garden door opens suddenly and* MORGAN *appears.*)

MORGAN. I caught the early train. (*Puts bag above large desk* R.) I knew they would all be watching for me, so I got out at Llanmorfedd and got a lift to Gwaenygam.

MISS MOFFAT. Does that mean ——?

MORGAN. Oh, no news. (*He puts down his bag and cap.*) Except that I am not hopeful. (*Crosses to armchair* R. C.)

MISS MOFFAT. Why not?

MORGAN. They talked to me for one hour at the Viva ——

MISS MOFFAT. That doesn't mean anything. Go on. (*Crosses, sits* L. *end of couch.*)

MORGAN. They jumped down hard on the New Testament question. As you said they would —(*A step* L.)—you are very pale.

MISS MOFFAT. Better than a raging fever. Go on.

MORGAN. (*Sits armchair* R. C.) I spent five minutes explaining why Saint Paul sailed from a town three hundred miles inland.

MISS MOFFAT. Oh, dear. (MORGAN'S *English has immensely improved, and he expresses himself with ease.*) Parnell?

MORGAN. Parnell . . . (*Smiles.*) Oh, yes—I was going to stick up for the old chap, but when they started off with " that fellow Parnell," I told the tale against him for half an hour. I wasn't born a Welshman for nothing.

MISS MOFFAT. Ha . . . And the French?

MORGAN. Not good. I said " naturellement " to everything, but it didn't fit every time.

MISS MOFFAT. And the Greek verbs?

MORGAN. They were sarcastic.

MISS MOFFAT. Did the President send for you?

MORGAN. I had half an hour with him ——

MISS MOFFAT. You did?

MORGAN. Yes, but so did the other nine candidates! He was a very kind and grand old gentleman sitting in a drawing-room the size of Penlan Town Hall. I talked about religion, the same as you said ——

MISS MOFFAT. Just as you advised ——

MORGAN. Just as you advised. He asked me if I had ever had strong drink, and I looked him straight in the eye and said " No."

MISS MOFFAT. Oh!

MORGAN. I was terrible—terribly nervous. My collar stud flew off, and I had to hold on to my collar with one hand, and he did not seem impressed with me at all. . . . He was very curious about you. (*Rises.*) Did you know there was an article in the Morning Post about the school?

MISS MOFFAT. Was there? . . . But what else makes you despondent?

MORGAN. The other candidates. They appeared to be brilliant— I had never thought they would be, somehow! Two from Eton and one from Harrow, one of them very rich. I had never thought a scholarship man might be rich. He had his own servant.

MISS MOFFAT. Gosh!

MORGAN. And the servant looked so like my father I thought it was at first . . . (*Crosses upstage* R. *of small desk* L. C.) And as I was leaving, the examiners appeared to be sorry for me in some way, and I received the impression that I had failed. I ——

MISS MOFFAT. When shall we know?

MORGAN. The day after tomorrow. They are writing to you.

MISS MOFFAT.. The villagers (*Rises, crosses* R. *to above* R. C. *armchair.*) are all in their best, and talking about a holiday tomorrow. It is very stupid of them, because if you have failed it will make you still more sick at heart ——

MORGAN. If I have failed? (*Crosses via* C. *to front of couch.*) Don't speak about it!

MISS MOFFAT. But we must! You faced the idea the day you left for Oxford ——

70

MORGAN. I know, but I have *been* to Oxford, and come back, since then! I have come back—from the world! Since the day I was born, I have been a prisoner behind (*Sits* L. *end of couch.*) a stone wall, and now somebody has given me a leg-up to have a look at the other side . . . they cannot drag me back again, they cannot, they *must* give me a push and send me over!

MISS MOFFAT. (*Crosses, sits* R. *of couch.*) I've never heard you talk so much since I've known you.

MORGAN. That is just it! I *can* talk, now! The three days I have been there, I have been talking my head off!

MISS MOFFAT. Ha! If three days at Oxford can do that to you, what would you be like at the end of three years?

MORGAN. That's just it again—it would be everything I need, everything! Starling and I spent three hours one night discussin' the law—Starling, you know, the brilliant one. . . . The words came pouring out of me—all the words that I had learnt and written down and never spoken—I suppose I was talking nonsense, but I was at least holding a conversation! I suddenly realized that I had never done it before—I had never been *able* to do it. (*With a strong Welsh accent.*) " How are you, Morgan? Nice day, Mr. Jones! Not bad for the harvest! "—a vocabulary of twenty words; all the thoughts that you have given to me were being stored away as if they were always going to be useless—locked up and rotting away—a lot of questions with nobody to answer them, a lot of statements with nobody to contradict them . . . and there I was with Starling, nineteen to the dozen. I came out of his rooms that night, and I walked down the High. That's their High Street, you know.

MISS MOFFAT. Yes, yes. . . .

MORGAN. I looked up, and there was a moon behind Magd—Maudlin. Not the same moon I have seen over the Nant, a different face altogether. Everybody seemed to be walking very fast, with their gowns on, in the moonlight; the bells were ringing, and I was walking faster than anybody and I felt—well, the same as on the rum in the old days!

MISS MOFFAT. Go on.

MORGAN. All of a sudden, with one big rush, against that moon, and against that High Street . . . I saw this room; you and me sitting here studying, and all those books—and everything I have ever learnt from those books, and from you, was lighted up—like a magic lantern—ancient Rome, Greece, Shakespeare, Carlyle,

71

Milton . . . everything had a meaning because I was in a new world—my world! And so it came to me why you worked like a slave to make me ready for this scholarship . . . I've finished.

MISS MOFFAT. I didn't want you to stop.

MORGAN. I had not been drinking.

MISS MOFFAT. I know.

MORGAN. I can talk to you too, now.

MISS MOFFAT. Yes. I'm glad. (SQUIRE *comes in from front door.* MORGAN *rises, back* L. *of step.*)

SQUIRE. No sign of the feller-me-lad, dang it —— (*Hangs hat on door.*) Evans! (*Crosses to* MORGAN *down* L., *shakes hands.*) There you are! . . .

MORGAN. Good day, sir.

SQUIRE. Well?

MORGAN. They are sending the result through the post.

SQUIRE. The devil they are. (*To* MISS MOFFAT—*crosses* R., *sits armchair at* R. C. MISS MOFFAT *crosses to desk* R.) D'ye know I am finding this waiting a definite strain? . . . (JONES *runs in from study, stops at foot of stairs.*)

JONES. Somebody said they had seen Morgan ——

MORGAN. Day after tomorrow. (*Sits settle* L.)

JONES. Oh . . . (*Crosses via* L. *to up* C. *blackboard.*)

SQUIRE. Examiners all right, my boy?

MORGAN. Rather sticky, sir.

SQUIRE. Lot of old fogies, I expect. Miss Moffat, (*Turns to her.*) I told you you ought to have made inquiries at the other place. However . . . (MISS RON. *runs in from study—stops* L.)

MISS RON. Somebody said they had seen ——

SQUIRE and JONES. The day after tomorrow!

MISS RON. Oh . . . How are you, Morgan, dear . . . (*Crosses via front to large desk* R. *below it.*)

JONES. The suspense is terrible. (JONES *crosses up to door, looks* R. MISS MOFFAT *crosses to alcove up* C.)

SQUIRE I know.

JONES. Even the little children are worrying about —— (*Closes door. He comes into room, crosses in to* L. *of blackboard.*) Morgan, my boy . . . are you not exhausted after your journey— would you not like something to eat?

MORGAN I am rather hungry, yes ——

MISS MOFFAT. But how stupid of me—Watty will boil you an egg —come along ——

MORGAN. (*Rises.*) Thank you—excuse me —— (*Follows* MISS MOFFAT *off.*)

MISS MOFFAT. (*As she goes into kitchen.*) Did they spot the Dryden howler?

MORGAN. No. (JONES *crosses to kitchen door, closes it, then crosses down* L. *of couch.*)

SQUIRE. You seemed very anxious to get 'em out of the room. What's the matter —— (*Front door opens and* BESSIE *walks in. She has completely changed, she might be ten years older. Her hair is up, she wears a cheaply smart costume, with a cape, and looks dazzlingly pretty in a loose opulent style. Her whole personality has blossomed. A pause. They stare at her.*)

BESSIE. Hello. (*Crosses down* R. C.)

SQUIRE. How d' ye do. . . .

BESSIE. I'm very well indeed, thanks, and how are you, (*To* SQUIRE.) blooming? (*Her accent is nearer the ladylike than it has yet been.*)

SQUIRE. Yes, thanks. . . . What *is* this?

MISS RON. I really couldn't say . . . (*Crosses in a step.*) Good gracious, it's Bessie W ——

BESSIE. Right first time. Hello, Miss Ronberry, how's geography, the world still goin' round in circles? Hello, (*Crosses to couch.*) Mr. Jones, flirty as ever?

SQUIRE. And to what do we owe this honor?

BESSIE. Well, it's like this —— (*Sits couch.*)

JONES. Miss Ronberry, will you please return to your class ——

MISS RON. They are quite safe. (*Crosses up to* R. *door.*) I left Mary Davies in charge ——

BESSIE. No, you don't. We've had too many secrets as it is —— (MISS RON. *crosses down to desk chair* R.)

JONES. Three days ago she sent money to you—did you not receive the letter ——

BESSIE. Yes, I did, and all the others, till I was sick of 'em.

SQUIRE. What *is* all this?

BESSIE. Last week I was glancing through the *Mid-Wales Gazette*, and I'm here to congratulate a certain young gent in case he has won that scholarship.

JONES. Oh!

MISS RON. But what has that got to do with you?

BESSIE. You see, Miss, it's like this ——

73

JONES. Don't say it—don't say it! (*Turns upstage away from her.*)

BESSIE. Four weeks yesterday, I had a baby. (*A pause.* MISS RON. *and* SQUIRE *stare at her.* JONES *gives a sigh of impotent despair.*)

SQUIRE. You had a what?

BESSIE. A baby. Seven pounds thirteen ounces. (MISS RON. *sits desk chair* R.)

SQUIRE. Good God, how ghastly!

JONES. (*Turns to her.*) It is a disgustin' subject and ——

BESSIE. It isn't disgusting at all; if I had a wedding ring you'd think it was sweet. (MRS. WATTY *hurries in from kitchen, crosses via back to above desk* R.—*picks up* MORGAN'S *suitcase.*)

MRS. WATTY. Morgan Evans's luggage. (*Starts* L.) Excuse me, sir. (*Catches sight of* SQUIRE'S *serious face.*) Oh! . . . Any news?

SQUIRE. Well, yes. . . .

MRS. WATTY. Bessie! (*Drops bag above couch,* R. *end.*) My, you do look a dollymop! Excuse me, sir. . . .

SQUIRE. Say anything you like ——

MRS. WATTY. (C. R. *of* BESSIE.) Where d'you get them bracelets?

BESSIE. Present.

MRS. WATTY. Oh, that's all right. Where 'ave you been, you Madam?

BESSIE. Turnin' you into a granny.

MRS. WATTY. A gra . . . (*Both laugh.*) Well, fancy! (MISS MOFFAT *comes in from kitchen.* JONES *crosses to front of steps.*)

MISS MOFFAT. And I should try and have a sleep if I were you —— (*Crosses down* L.)

MRS. WATTY. You could 'ave knocked me down with a feather!

BESSIE. Hello. I've just been telling them you-know-what.

SQUIRE. And now I think it's time you told us who the fellow is. I am going to take drastic proceedings ——

MRS. WATTY. That's right, dear—who is it ——

BESSIE. Well, as a matter of fact ——

MISS MOFFAT. (*To* L. *of couch.*) No! I'll pay you anything . . . anything!

BESSIE. It's no good, Miss. (MISS MOFFAT *turns away.*) It's Morgan Evans. (*A pause.*)

SQUIRE. What!

MISS RON. (*Rises.*) I don't believe it. . . .

MRS. WATTY. Oh, Ma'am. (*Crosses up back of double desk above couch.*)

74

MISS MOFFAT. I've been dreading this for months. In a terrible way it's a relief.

BESSIE. Bamboozlin' me every week he was, in the gutter!

MISS MOFFAT. Lies, all lies, and I was glad to be telling them —— (*Goes to settle, below stairway.* MRS. WATTY *crosses,* C. *above and* R. *of* IDWAL'S *desk.*)

MISS RON. I can't go on listening! I can't bear it! It all comes of meddling with this teaching—she was in my class—(*Sits desk chair* R.)—what *would* Papa have said! This horrible unnatural happening ——

MISS MOFFAT. Don't talk nonsense, it isn't horrible, and it isn't unnatural! On the contrary, it's nature giving civilization a nasty tweak of the nose. (*Sits settle.*) The schoolmistress has learnt a lesson, but it's a little late now.

BESSIE. (*Rises, crosses to up* C.) Where is he?

MRS. WATTY. Over my dead body, my girl ——

BESSIE. (*To* R. *of* MRS. WATTY.) She's right, Mum, it's too late, I got a four-weeks-old baby, kickin' healthy and hungry, and I haven't got a husband to keep him, so his father's got to turn *into* my husband. That's only fair, (*Crosses to* C. *again.*) isn't it?

SQUIRE. (*Rises.*) I'm sorry, Miss Moffat, but I'm inclined to agree —— (*Crosses halfway up to* R. U. *door.*)

BESSIE. I'll call him —— (*Starts* L.)

JONES. There is no need to call him!

SQUIRE. What's the matter with you?

JONES. (*A step forward.*) I am sorry to say that I have a strong feeling of affection for this young woman.

BESSIE. Oh, yes—(*Crosses front of couch.*)—I've got the face of an angel, haven't I?

JONES. And I am willing to do my duty by rehabilitating her in wedlock, (BESSIE *sits* C. *of couch.*) and bestowing on the infant every advantage by bringing it up a Baptist.

SQUIRE. Are you serious? (*Comes downstage.*)

JONES. I am always serious.

BESSIE. (*To* MISS MOFFAT.) You'd like that, wouldn't you?

MRS. WATTY. (*Crosses down* R. *of couch.*) Now we're not pretendin' it's a windfall, but for a girl who's took the wrong turnin' it's a present! And you'd 'ave your own way in everything—wouldn't she, sir?

JONES. Of course ——

MRS. WATTY. Well, will you?

BESSIE. No. I won't. I'd like to oblige . . . (*Laughs.*) but really I couldn't! (JONES *turns away.*) Besides, my friend would be furious.

MRS. WATTY. Your friend?

BESSIE. Ever such a nice gentleman, sporting, quite a swell, owns a race-course. (MRS. WATTY *looks suspicious.*) You needn't look like that, I only met him ten weeks ago. (MRS. WATTY *crosses up* R. *of small desk.*) I'd started servin' behind a bar for fun, I was the picture of health and ever so lucky in the counter bein' very high.

SQUIRE. I have never heard such a conversation outside a police court. I am seeking the safety of my own quarters—(*Crosses up to* R. *upper door.*)—anything I can do, Miss Moffat ——

BESSIE. I suppose *you* wouldn't care to stake a claim?

SQUIRE. Good gracious —— (*Exits* R. U. *door.* BESSIE *laughs.*)

MISS MOFFAT. Doesn't this man of yours want to marry you?

BESSIE. 'E won't talk of anything else, but he won't have the baby. He says it would be different if the father'd been a pal of his— you can understand it, really, can't you? (MISS MOFFAT *crosses up* L. *to alcove.*) So I've got to give up my friend and marry Morgan Evans. Pity, 'cos my friend worships me. Ever since I left he keeps on sending me telegrams. I just got two at the station, and I expect I'll get some more tonight, isn't it rich? (*Laughs.*) Mr. Jones wouldn't consider the baby without me?

MISS RON. The baby without you! Your child! What about your— your mother love?

BESSIE. I expect you'll think I'm a wicked girl, but d'you know, I haven't got any!

MISS RON. Oh, what a vile thing to say, vile ——

BESSIE. (*Rises, crosses to* MISS RON. *to* L. *of her.*) Now listen, dear . . . you're seeing this baby as if it was yours, aren't you— you'd think the world of it, wouldn't you?

MISS RON. It would mean everything to me . . . (*Turns away.*) my whole life . . .

BESSIE. I have a pretty near idea how old you are! When I'm your age I'll love the idea of a baby, but life hasn't begun yet for me—I'm just getting a taste for it—(*Crosses* C.)—what do *I* want with a baby?

MRS. WATTY. That's what we all want to know!

BESSIE. Yes, Mum, but you know what it is ——

MISS RON. You're inhuman, (*Rises, crosses front to* L. *first.* MRS. WATTY *crosses up to* R. *end of alcove.*) that's what you are! To think you don't want it. . . . (*Exits* L. 1—*runs last few steps.*)

BESSIE. I didn't mean to be nasty—but inhuman indeed! (*Crosses* R. *above armchair* R. C.) I didn't (*Crosses down* R.) want the baby, nobody would have, but I was careful so it'd (*Crosses* C.) be all right, and now it is all right I want it to have a good time—but *I* want a good time too! I *could* have left (*Above chair* R.) it on a door-step, couldn't I? But I must see it's in good hands—and that's why I've come to Morgan Evans.

MISS MOFFAT. (*Crosses down to* L. *of* BESSIE.) You want to make him marry you, on the chance he will become fond enough of the child to ensure its future—your conscience will be clear and later you can go off on your own?

BESSIE. I shouldn't be surprised ——

MISS MOFFAT. In the meantime, it's worth while to ruin a boy on —on the threshold of ——

BESSIE. I don't know anything about that, I'm sure. (*Calling.*) Morgan!

MISS MOFFAT. Ssh! Wait a minute, wait. . . . There may be a way out—there must be ——

MRS. WATTY. (*To* L. *of* MISS MOFFAT.) Gawd bless us, Ma'am—I got it!

MISS MOFFAT. What?

MRS. WATTY. Why can't you adopt it? (JONES *takes a step forward.*)

MISS MOFFAT. Don't be ridiculous.

MRS. WATTY. Would that do you, Bessie?

BESSIE. Well! I never thought . . .

MRS. WATTY. Would it, though?

BESSIE. Yes, it would.

MISS MOFFAT. It *would*? . . . But . . . but what would *I* do with a baby? I—I don't even know what they look like!

MRS. WATTY. They're lovely little things—now it's all arranged ——

MISS MOFFAT. But it would be fantastic —— (*Crosses to* R. *of couch,* L. MRS. WATTY *crosses* R. *of armchair* R. C.)

BESSIE. (*Crosses down* R. *of* MISS MOFFAT.) Oh, do, please, it'd put *everything* to rights! I would know the baby was safe, Morgan Evans need never know a thing about it, I can marry my friend, and it will all be beautiful! He might grow like his father

77

and turn out quite nice, and anyway I'm not really so bad, you know—and he's on the bottle now—and I could give all the instructions before I go—and you could have it straight away, see, because if it's going I don't want to have it with me longer than I can help, see, because I'd only start gettin' fond of it, see ——

MRS. WATTY. Come on, Ma'am, you've been pushin' us about for three years, now we'll give *you* a shove!

MISS MOFFAT. But it's mad—I tell you ——

MRS. WATTY. Not as mad as takin' *me* in was, with my trouble! You've allus been like that, you might as well go on ——

MISS MOFFAT. (*Crosses to* C. *of couch.*) But I was never meant to be a mother—I'm not like Miss Ronberry—why, *she* is the one to do it ——

JONES. (*Crosses in to* L. *of couch.*) She would never agree—we were discussin' Marged Hopkins going to the workhouse—and she said she could never hold with any child born like that.

MISS MOFFAT. Oh . . . I suppose it would worry some folk. . . . (*Crosses* R. *to* L. *of armchair* R. C). But, Watty, you're the grandmother, and surely you ——

MRS. WATTY. Oh, I couldn't! I don't bear it no ill-will, but every penny I get goes to the Corpse. You're the one, dear, really you are.

MISS MOFFAT. (*Crosses to* R. *of* BESSIE.) Bessie Watty, do you mean that if I do not adopt this child, you ——

BESSIE. I will have to tell Morgan Evans, and he will have to marry me, I swear that.

MISS MOFFAT. And do you swear that you would never let Morgan Evans know the truth?

BESSIE. I swear. If there are any questions, I'll say it was my friend's. (*A pause.*)

MISS MOFFAT. Then . . . I give in. (*Sits armchair at* R. C.)

BESSIE. That's lovely. My friend will be pleased. (*Crosses up to* R.) I'll pop back to the public-house for his telegram and send him a nice one back. Good-bye, all, we'll arrange details later, shall we? (*Crosses back,* C. *to above* MRS. WATTY.) My friend gave me this buckle, isn't it nice? He offered me a tiny one, real, but I think the false is prettier, don't you?

JONES. (L. *of couch.*) Are you going to take up a life of sin?

BESSIE. (*Crosses* C.) I shouldn't be surprised. (JONES 2 *steps up* L.) I'm only really meself with a lot of gentlemen round me, y'know, and a nice glass o' port will never come amiss, neither.

(*Crosses* R. C. *a step.*) That cold water didn't really do the trick, Mum, did it? . . . (MRS. WATTY *gestures to her.*) Good-bye . . . (*Crosses* C.) I only did it to spite you, y'know.

JONES. You are not fit to touch the hem of her garment.

BESSIE. Oh, yes, I am! Just because she's read a lot o' books. (*Crosses upstage.*) Books, books! . . . Look at 'em all! I got more out of life at my age than she has out o' them all her days —and I'll get a lot more yet! What d'you bet me? (*She goes out by front door, leaves door open.* MRS. WATTY *crosses up, closes door.*)

MRS. WATTY. That's settled . . . (*Comes down. The voices of children in the barn, singing " Dacw'n-ghariad.*")

JONES. For which we must be truly thankful. . . . (*Crosses to below stairs.* MORGAN *walks in quickly from kitchen.*)

MORGAN. Has she gone? (*Crosses via back to* C. *above small desk.*)

MISS MOFFAT. Why?

MORGAN. The Squire just came in to see me.

MISS MOFFAT. The fool! The idiotic fool —— (MRS. WATTY *crosses to window.*)

MORGAN. Then it's true! . . . (*Steps toward her. A pause.*) He thought I knew. (*Laughs.*) Then he said it was for the best—that I ought to be told . . . (*Singing stops in barn.*) It is funny. She and I, we do not know each other at all—it was a long time ago, and I never thought again about it—and neither did she, I know she didn't . . . and here we are. . . . (*Crosses to above desk chair* R.) It is funny, too, because if you and I had not made that bad quarrel, it would never have happened. . . . It ought to make me feel older . . . but I feel more—young than I have ever done before. . . . (*Turns* R.) Oh, God, why should this happen? . . .

MISS MOFFAT. Steady . . .

JONES. (*A step forward.*) There is no need for you to upset yourself, my boy. Miss Moffat is going to take care of—of ——

MORGAN. What? (*Turns.*)

MISS MOFFAT. I am going to adopt it.

MORGAN. What in hell do you take me for?

JONES. Morgan, swearing! Be haru ti ——

MORGAN. I will (*Crosses to* R. *end of couch via front.*) swear some more too, if people talk to me like that! What do you take me for?

JONES. (*Two steps to him.*) Then what yould you like to do, my boy —— (MRS. WATTY *crosses to single desk up* L.)

MORGAN. What would I like to do? (*To* R. *of* JONES. *Getting more*

79

and more Welsh.) It is not a question of what I would like to do, or what I might be allowed but what I am *going* to do—what any fellow with any guts in him must do! (*Crosses up* R.) I am going to marry her!

MISS MOFFAT. (*With a cry, rises,—crosses to* R. *of couch.*) I knew this would happen, I knew ——

MORGAN. What else is there, when I have made a fool of myself and of her, and of the poor—(*Up* R. *above desk.*)—the poor—I am not going to talk about any of it to anybody, all I will say is that Bessie Watty and I are going to get married as soon as we can, and that is final!

MISS MOFFAT. I see. (*Sits couch.* SARAH *hurries in.* MRS. WATTY *down to* L. *of her.*)

SARAH. Bessie's telegram from her friend, they send it from Penlan—I never seed one before!

MRS. WATTY. Poor chap, 'e'll be disappointed again. . . . (*Opens telegram, hands it to* MISS MOFFAT.) What does it say, Ma'am? . . . Read it, Ma'am, take your mind off things. . . .

MISS MOFFAT. "You have won the scholarship." (*Reading.*) "First, Evans, Second, Fayver-Giles, Third, Starling. Congratulations." (SARAH *claps her hands and runs out by front door, closes it.* MORGAN *laughs bitterly.*) Lock the school door, Watty, will you?

MRS. WATTY. (*Crosses via front to door* L. 1.) Go in there, sir, I'll make you a cup of tea. . . . (JONES *goes into kitchen.* MRS. WATTY *locks study door and follows him.*)

MISS MOFFAT. Look at me, Morgan. (*He crosses in 2 steps.* MORGAN *faces her in armchair, defiantly.*) For the first time, we are together. Our hearts are face to face, naked and unashamed, because there's no time to lose, my boy; the clock is ticking and there's no time to lose. If ever anybody has been at the crossroads, you are now ——

MORGAN. It is no good. (*Crosses down* R.) I am going to marry her.

MISS MOFFAT. And I am going to speak to you very simply. I want you to change suddenly from a boy to a man. I understand that this is a great shock to you, but I want you to throw off this passionate obstinacy to do the right thing. . . . Did you promise her marriage?

MORGAN. No, never —— (*Turns* R.)

80

MISS MOFFAT. Did you even tell her that you were in love with her?

MORGAN. No, never ——

MISS MOFFAT. Then your situation now is the purest accident; it is to be regretted, but it has happened before and it will happen again. So cheer up, you are not the central figure of such a tragedy as you think ——

MORGAN. (*Crosses 2 steps* L.) That does not alter the fact that I have a duty to—to them both ——

MISS MOFFAT. She has her own plans, and she doesn't want the child; and I am willing to look after it if you behave as I want you to behave. If you marry her, you know what will happen, don't you? You will go back to the mine. In a year she will have left you—both. You will be drinking again, and this time you will not stop. And you will enjoy being this besotted and uncouth village genius who once showed such promise; but it will not be worth it, you know.

MORGAN. (*Crosses front of* R. C. *armchair.*) There is a child, living and breathing on this earth, and living and breathing because of me ——

MISS MOFFAT. I don't care if there are fifty children on this earth because of you! . . . (MORGAN *sits armchair* R. C.) You mentioned the word " duty," did you? Yes, you have a duty, but it is not to this loose little lady, or to her offspring either.

MORGAN. You mean a duty to you?

MISS MOFFAT. No. A year ago I should have said a duty to me, yes; but that night you showed your teeth . . . you gave me a lot to think about, you know. You caught me unawares, and I gave you the worst possible answer back; I turned sorry for myself and taunted you with ingratitude. I was a dolt not to realize that a debt of gratitude is the most humiliating debt of all, and that a little show of affection would have wiped it out. I offer that affection to you, today.

MORGAN. Why are you saying this to me now?

MISS MOFFAT. Because, as the moments are passing, and I am going to get my way, I know that I am never going to see you again. (*A pause.*)

MORGAN. Never again? But why?

MISS MOFFAT. If you are not to marry her, it would be madness for you to come into contact with the child; so if I am adopting the child, you can never come to see me; it is common sense. You have been given the push over the wall that you asked for.

MORGAN. But you . . . will be staying here—how can I never come back—after everything you have done for me?

MISS MOFFAT. D'you remember, the last six months, I've gone for a long walk over Moel Hiraeth, every morning at eight, like clockwork, for my health?

MORGAN. Yes?

MISS MOFFAT. There's one bit of the road, round a boulder—and there's an oak-tree, and under it the valley suddenly drops sheer. Every morning regularly, as I was turning that corner, by some trick of the mind, I found myself thinking of you working for this scholarship, and winning it. And I experienced something which must after all be comparatively rare: A feeling . . . of complete happiness. I shall experience it again. No, Morgan Evans, you have no duty to me. Your only duty—is to the world.

MORGAN. To the world?

MISS MOFFAT. Now you are going, there is no harm in telling you something. I don't think you realize quite what your future can become if you give it the chance. I have always been very definite about the things I wanted, and I have always had everything worked out to a T—p'r'aps that's the trouble with me, I dunno . . . I've got *you* worked out, and it's up to you whether it will come right or not ——

MORGAN. Go on.

MISS MOFFAT. I rather made out to the Squire that I wanted you to be a writer—the truth might have sounded ridiculous; but stranger things have happened. You have brains, shrewdness, eloquence, and imagination; and Oxford will give you enough of the graces.

MORGAN. For what?

MISS MOFFAT. Maybe to become a great man of our country. " If a light come in the mine " you said, remember?

MORGAN. Yes.

MISS MOFFAT. Make that light come in the mine and some day free these children. And you could be more, much, much more, you could be a man for a future nation to be proud of. . . . Perhaps I'm mad, I dunno, we'll see. It's up to you.

MORGAN. (*Rises before speaking.*) Yes. (JONES *appears timidly from kitchen.*)

JONES. Is it all right to ring the bell to say holiday tomorrow? (*He comes down* L.)

MISS MOFFAT. Yes. (*She smiles.* JONES *smiles. His face lights up, he hurries to study door, unlocks it, and disappears.* MISS MOFFAT *rises.*) I think that's all.

MORGAN. But—I—I do not know what to say.

MISS MOFFAT. Then don't say it. (*He turns, looks upstage.*)

MORGAN. I have been . . . (*A step up.*) so much time in this room.

MISS MOFFAT. And the lessons are over.

MORGAN. (*A step to her.*) I shall—always remember. .

MISS MOFFAT. Will you? Well, I'm glad you think you will. (*Gets bag from front of small desk.* MORGAN *crosses to her, she gives him the bag.* IDWAL *runs in from study, very excited, to below stairs.* ROBBART *appears downstage of him.*)

IDWAL. Please, Miss Moffat, the band is out, and they say Morgan got to come down to Penlan Town Hall for Wales to see a real toff!

MORGAN. Na, ddim diolch ——

ROBBART. Tyd, man, tyd, they never forgive you! (*An afterthought.*) And please, Miss Moffat, Mr. Jones say is he to say school day after tomorrow, nine o'clock same as usual?

MISS MOFFAT. Nine o'clock. The same as usual. . . .

ROBBART. Yes, Miss Moffat. (*He runs back into study, followed by* IDWAL.)

MISS MOFFAT. (*She offers her hand, he takes it.*) Good-bye. And I had my heart set on coming up to London and having tea on the Terrace. (VOICES *mixed with singing off-stage.*)

IDWAL. (*Putting his head round the barn door, and disappearing again.*) Brysia, Morgan Evans, brysia! (MORGAN *tries to say something, fails, and hurries into study.* MISS MOFFAT *crosses to desk below desk chair. The kitchen door opens, and* MRS. WATTY *appears cautiously.*)

MRS. WATTY. (*Whispering.*) Has he gone? (*Crosses to* L. *of* MISS MOFFAT.)

MISS MOFFAT. Yes. It's all over.

MRS. WATTY. Bessie's sent a gentleman over to see you from the public-house —— (*Hands her birth certificate.*)

MISS MOFFAT. Tell him I can't see anybody —— (*Taking certificate.*) What's this?

MRS. WATTY. His birth certificate, Ma'am.

MISS MOFFAT. I had forgotten—all about that. (MRS. WATTY *starts to kitchen.*)

MRS. WATTY. (*At back of desk up* C.) Come on, Ma'am, you got to start some time! (*Crosses* L. *to exit.*)

MISS MOFFAT. Just coming. (MRS. WATTY *goes into kitchen. The sound of the village* PEOPLE *singing and cheering down the road. A pause.* MISS MOFFAT *looks down at birth certificate. The singing and cheering die down and stop. A pause.*) Moffat, my girl, you mustn't be clumsy this time. You mustn't be clumsy . . . (*The school bell begins to ring, clear and confident. She looks up, as she did once before, listening, smiling faintly. A vociferous burst of cheering in the village. She turns and walks toward the kitchen.*)

CURTAIN

PROPERTY PLOT

ACT I—SCENE 1

Furniture

Flat top desk
1—Desk chair
1—Centre table (domes on it to slide easily)
1—Armchair (domes on it to slide easily)
1—Sofa
1—Welsh sideboard (plates and crockery)
1—Settle
1—Small table in window recess
1—Grandfather clock
Book shelves—2 sets on R. wall. Back wall covered from door R. to alcove—all filled with real books
1—Small stool
1—Step ladder
Waste paper basket
1—Chair at up R. C.
1—Chair at up L.
2—Rugs (alike)
Curtains to close on alcove windows—none on R. windows

Off Front Door

2—Wrapped, cloth covered parcels of books (Mrs. Watty)
Brown paper parcels (Bessie)
A hamper with books, several articles tied together with rope (Mrs. Watty)
Bicycle (lady's) (Miss Moffat)
A satchel on a shoulder strap (sheafs of papers) (Miss Moffat)

Off Kitchen

Tea tray, 3 cups, saucers, creamer, spoons. Tea service, sugar bowl
Enormous teapot

Off Garden

Bunch of flowers (Idwal)

On Sofa

Books, cushions

At R. Below Desk

Packing case with 5 books, small stool

On Seat Below Stairs

Sewing basket, pin cushion, pins, needles, one threaded needle
Pair gloves
Lady's parasol

On Table in Alcove

Vase for flowers—6 books

On Table C.

Cloth

On Window Seat

Books

On Desk

Writing pad, desk set, pens, scissors

Hand Props

Rum bottle ¾ full—(Morgan) (small)
Tiny lace handkerchief (Miss Ronberry)

Dust rag (Mr. Jones)
English penny (Squire)

ON CHAIR R. C.

Packing case and 1 book

ON SIDEBOARD

China plates

5—Pewter pieces
4—Silver spoons
4—Pewter plates
Cups, saucers
1—Silver ash tray
1—China tureen
1—China sugar bowl

ACT I—SCENE 2

The same—six weeks later. Window curtains closed.
Armchair pushed R. of desk.

1—Small bench (4 ft. long, 11½ inches wide)
1—Small bench R. (4 ft. 6 in. long, 11½ in. wide)
Red geraniums in pots across the window sill
Miss Moffat's straw hat on knob of settle, at foot of stairs
The big desk, the desk chair, the sofa and the settle are littered with exercise books and sheets of paper
Waste paper basket under table C.

ON TABLE L. C.

8—Grubby books (exercise)—one on top of the other in leather tray

All kinds of assorted papers on settle
Many papers and books (on desk)
Leather desk tray full of papers (on desk R.)
Waste basket under table C.
A bell offstage for school bell effect
Rack off stage for bell

ON DESK

Exercise books and essay papers

1—Essay book with a crude drawing of a lady in bicycle bloomers

OFF KITCHEN

Cup of tea—spoon
Bucket full of soap suds

OFF UPSTAIRS

Roll of papers (Miss Moffat) (long roll—she uses them to spank Morgan)

OFF UP R.

Small wooden crate that opens on the side with a small monastery bell with rope—(about a cubic foot in size)—papier-mâché

OFF GARDEN

Lighted oil (fake) lantern

OFF UPSTAIRS

Basket of washing
Chair and clothes rack for quick change
Handkerchief (Miss Ronberry)

OFF KITCHEN

Books (for Mr. Jones)

Bag of sweeties—printing on bag (Bessie)
A mailed (English stamped) letter, with a written letter inside

OFF STUDY
Arithmetic (Miss Ronberry)

HAND PROPS
Rum bottle—½ pint (Morgan)

ACT II—SCENE 1
The same—two years later. Early evening—sunlight.

The table in the recess is replaced by two school desks
The recess table and small chair are pushed behind sofa
A school desk is between the big desk and sofa
Two rows of 4 school desks each
Stool at between sofa and foot of stairs—a ruler (Miss Ronberry)
The lamp has been removed from table to upstage
Potted plants on window sills

ON WALLS
Charts, maps, an alphabet list, pinned up over the books
Hat pegs on
Books on dresser in place of plates
A hook on the back of the front door with Miss Moffat's cloak
A blackboard lies against the sofa with "Constantinople is the capital of Turkey" written on the blackboard

ON DESK
Exercise papers and pencils

AT BOOKCASE DOWN R.
Essay on Man (Pope)
Book of Shakespeare

ON SCHOOL DESKS
Slates and slate pencils and 1 book

ON TABLE L.
Small Greek dictionary
2—Mailed tradesman bills on desk R.
Small hand bell on table L.
Pumice stone in drawer of dresser
Small mirror placed in space in bookcase down R.

OFF GARDEN
Exercise book (Grammar)

OFF STUDY
9—Ink written sheets
Pen
1—Ink written sheet
1—Pen, books, papers, exercise book (Morgan)

OFF FRONT DOOR R.
Lady's umbrella
Brown paper parcel

OFF KITCHEN
Cup of water
Milk jug and a cup

OFF STAIR LANDING
Lady's hair brush
Door bang

A door key
1—Towel
1—Bowl of roses
Morgan's cap on peg on scene
  —above door L. 1

Blackboard—rag at board
Rum bottle (Morgan)
Rag eraser at board

ACT II—SCENE 2
The same—three months later. The potted plants
removed.

Desk seat, chair up R.
Waste paper basket up R.
Foolscap paper

NEAR FRONT DOOR ON FLOOR
A mailed English written letter
  (to be opened)
1—Mailed letter with English
  birth certificate
    IN DRAWER OF DESK
Paper parcel tied with a string,
  with assorted papers in it
Foolscap paper
An official (mailed envelope)
  with the examination questions from Oxford, with a duplicate copy
Letter opener

OFF KITCHEN
A small table (new and light
  with blotter, ink, ink-stand,
  pen, pencil)

A duster
A cup of tea—spoon
A steaming cup and saucer—
  spoon (tea)

OFF STUDY
The stage R. C. armchair (inside
  door)

OFF UP R.
Snow mixture (to sprinkle on
  characters)
Straw bag (Bessie)
Several English periodicals, most
  of them sporting and dramatic (Old)
Clock strike — Grandfather's
  clock

HAND PROPS
Spray of white heather (Miss
  Ronberry)
Pencil and note paper on desk

ACT III
The same—July, seven months later.

The small table is back in recess
The armchair is in its old posi-
  tion
The large table centre struck
3—Small school desks in its place
  (1 single—1 double)
Blackboard on an easel with
  "Elizabeth, known as Good

Q. Bess" written on it in
  block letters
Slate and pencil at each desk
Slate and pencil on settle
Arithmetic papers on dresser, and
  book, chalk and cloth at
  blackboard
School bell cues in this act
Key in lock of study door

On Large Desk

Large bottle of ink in drawer (lower drawer)
Row of ink wells on lower end
Small square satchel full of school papers

At Each Desk

4—School books
1—Slate and pencil
1—Book strap (three sets of these)

On Sideboard

Small ship
Globe top bookcase
Books off top sideboard
Lamp on sideboard
Take half books off top of bookcase
Small horse

Off Garden

School papers and several books

Off Study

Exercise book
Handkerchief (Miss Moffat)
Sheet of music

Off Up r.

Traveling bag (Morgan)
Sealed English telegram

Off Kitchen

English birth certificate

Hand Props

Mouth organ (Robbart)
Watch (Miss Moffat) (to pin on waist)
Bracelets (Bessie)

NEW
PLAYS

THE AFRICAN COMPANY PRESENTS RICHARD III
by Carlyle Brown

EDWARD ALBEE'S
FRAGMENTS and THE MARRIAGE PLAY

IMAGINARY LIFE
by Peter Parnell

MIXED EMOTIONS
by Richard Baer

THE SWAN
by Elizabeth Egloff

Write for information as to
availability
DRAMATISTS PLAY SERVICE, Inc.
440 Park Avenue South   New York, N.Y. 10016

NEW
PLAYS

THE LIGHTS
by Howard Korder

THE TRIUMPH OF LOVE
by James Magruder

LATER LIFE
by A.R. Gurney

THE LOMAN FAMILY PICNIC
by Donald Margulies

A PERFECT GANESH
by Terrence McNally

SPAIN
by Romulus Linney

*Write for information as to
availability*
DRAMATISTS PLAY SERVICE, Inc.
440 Park Avenue South   New York, N.Y. 10016

NEW
PLAYS

LONELY PLANET
by Steven Dietz

THE AMERICA PLAY
by Suzan-Lori Parks

THE FOURTH WALL
by A.R. Gurney

JULIE JOHNSON
by Wendy Hammond

FOUR DOGS AND A BONE
by John Patrick Shanley

DESDEMONA, A PLAY ABOUT A
HANDKERCHIEF
by Paula Vogel

*Write for information as to
availability*
DRAMATISTS PLAY SERVICE, Inc.
440 Park Avenue South   New York, N.Y. 10016